Richard McNicol

SOUND
inventions

32 creative music projects for the junior classroom

Music Department
OXFORD UNIVERSITY PRESS
Oxford and New York

© Oxford University Press 1992

OXFORD is a trade mark of Oxford University Press

First published 1992
Reprinted 1995, 1997
ISBN 0 19 321 432 6

Printed in China

Acknowledgements

Designed by Design Locker

Illustrations by John Craig

Photographs:
Collections/Brian Shuel, London p.112
Garden Photo Library, London p.10 left
Sally and Richard Greenhill, London p.18 right
Robert Harding Picture Library, London p.97
Michael Holford, Loughton, Essex p.10 centre, p.59 left, centre, p.61
Hulton Picture Company, London p.18 left, centre
Frank Lane Agency, Stowmarket p.14
Magnum, London p.67
Network, London p.56
Oxford Scientific Films, Oxford p.11, p.25, p.94
Oxford University Press p.20 top, p.15, p.33
Popperfoto, London p.30, p.57, p.59 right
Linda Proud, Oxford p.10 right, p.20 bottom, p.28

Contents

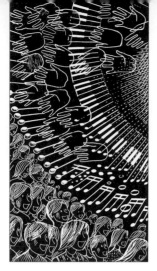

INTRODUCTION

Guide for class teachers

The aim of making music together is to enjoy it. This book contains thirty-two creative music projects that I have found exciting, stimulating, and fun to do with primary school children.

What is the aim of the book?

When first devising these projects I made myself one important rule: that I would avoid all the 'frighteners' that so disastrously persuaded many people of my generation that they were 'not musical' and 'couldn't do music'.

In these projects therefore:
- nobody needs to be able to read or write music
- nobody needs to be able to play an instrument
- no musical background of any sort is necessary.

My aim is to enable the primary class teacher to have the pleasure of exploring music with a class of children.

Will it be suitable for my class?

Every primary class contains children of widely varied ability. I have been careful to devise tasks capable of stretching the able, whilst stimulating both the less able and the child with learning difficulties (see p. 9).

Although this book explores many of the basic techniques of musical composition, it is not a *course* in musical invention. You are invited to dip into it where you will and to choose projects that you feel will suit your class.

You may, however, find that the first chapter, **Miniatures**, which deals with the simplest of musical concepts, is a good starting-point, while the last chapter, **Just imagine**, draws together some of the strands explored in earlier projects.

Working in groups

Music is a social activity and helps children, perhaps more than most other subjects, to develop skills that will be essential in later life:
- developing ideas
- working as a team
- discussing and negotiating
- leading and being led
- tolerating and supporting others
- presenting oneself in front of people.

For this reason I am a strong advocate of group work and have indicated throughout where I feel this to be appropriate.

Groups have practical advantages too; they provide more hands to put musical ideas into practice, and they bolster the confidence of the individuals within the group.

Group work can present some initial problems. Musical ideas cannot be explored without making sounds. And five groups of children working with voices and instruments in one room can generate a considerable amount of noise!

I find that a periodic review of work in progress (each group in turn showing what it has achieved whilst the rest of the class listens in silence) helps to keep the noise-level within manageable bounds.

Some practical points about working in groups

1 I like groups to sit on the floor. This allows children playing xylophones, metallophones, etc., to kneel behind the instruments with their hands at the correct height for playing. Xylophones on tables are invariably too high to play.

2 I encourage children to sit in a circle. This too is more easily done on the floor. Group work is about playing together and this can only satisfactorily be achieved when each member of the group can hear and *see* what everyone else is doing.

A circle also makes for easy discussion when the children are planning their music.

3 Teach the children to *begin* their music without 'counting in'. The sound of a child saying 'one, two, three, four' is a poor start to most pieces!
First teach the class to clap together:
- Put your hands together (as if in prayer).
- Ask the class to watch silently as, *with a continuous motion*, you clap once (starting and finishing in the prayer position).
- Now ask the class to make one clap with you. Make sure that everyone is watching you and that all hands are together. Then clap once. The clap will almost certainly be simultaneous — your parting hands act as a preparation which allows the children to gauge when the clap will come. This principle of physical preparation is precisely how pro-

fessional groups of musicians start together and how a conductor starts an orchestra.

- Now transfer the exercise onto an instrument. If you decide to start with a tambourine the motion will be identical to the clap. With a xylophone, start with the beater resting on the bar you are going to play (the equivalent of the hands together). Blown instruments are a little more difficult. Here the end of the instrument is lifted and returned to its starting position.

The secret is always to move continuously.

- Give the children a chance to practise in pairs, first one child leading, then the other.
- In a group the children will have to nominate a 'starter' — preferably someone whose first sound involves a good leading movement (a xylophone player, a drummer).

4 Be sure that the children know precisely what their task is before they divide into groups.

5 Encourage the children to try out their ideas quickly. We discover most easily what works and what doesn't by performing it, not by talking about it. And a group of children can discuss (and argue about) ideas all day long!

6 When groups perform to one another, remind the children that music starts and finishes *in silence*. I ask performing groups to wait until the listeners are absolutely silent before starting. Performance is a sharing in which performers have the responsibility of performing as well as possible and listeners have the responsibility of listening perfectly.

Is what my children invent really music?

It is perhaps impertinent of me to have included in the text so many warnings against imposing ideas on the children. It can be all too tempting for an enthusiastic teacher to invent a piece of music by instructing the children what to do! Children, like composers, must decide for themselves what they like and what they do not like. In music there are no absolute rights or wrongs; all is a matter for individual taste.

When children use sounds to invent music, it is important that they develop a musical language of their own. It is equally important that they have the opportunity to hear, enjoy, and understand the music of earlier ages and different cultures.

How do these projects fit into the National Curriculum?

The National Curriculum for England and Wales, revised in 1995, in essence requires children of ages 5 to 11 years to:

- use sounds, and to respond to music individually, in pairs, and in larger numbers.

- compose and improvise using their voices and instruments
- rehearse and perform songs, simple instrumental pieces and accompaniments, and record their music in various ways
- listen to and appraise a wide variety of music from different times and places, and by well known composers
- learn about the basic elements of music: pitch, duration, dynamics, tempo, timbre, texture, and structure

All the topics in this book contain these vital components of a child's musical education, and are designed so that the creative stimulus for each project can grow out of, lead into, or be combined with work in other areas of the curriculum.

This approach allows class teachers to use these projects with confidence, whatever their own level of musical skill might be.

How do I assess what the children are achieving?

In these projects the children learn to handle musical techniques by carrying out a series of tasks. As in any other subject, we assess the effectiveness and understanding with which these tasks have been tackled.

Visit each group in turn as the children work. You will soon get a clear idea of the contribution each child is making to the group. You may also need to even out the balance of power within some groups, gently making sure that each member has some say in what is going on.

When each group has performed its completed work to the class, help the children to discuss one another's work. Each child might also write a short assessment of his or her own contribution to the piece and an opinion of the effectiveness of the group's music.

Special sensitivity is required when we discuss the creative work of others. We all have our own personal pride in what we have created. Help the children to discuss one another's work in a constructive spirit of generosity.

Here are some questions we might ask ourselves or put to the class after listening to a performance:
- Did the piece have a specific aim—to amuse us, to frighten us, to describe something, to be really beautiful? Did it achieve this aim?
- Did the class feel that the piece was too long, too short, just right?
- Did it sound as if the players were playing at random or could some form of overall organization be detected? Can the children explain how they constructed their piece?
- Did the music contain contrasting sounds or did it sound the same all the way through? Was this what the children intended?
- Can the piece be performed again sounding substantially the same? (If it can, the children must have made specific decisions when organizing it.)

Children with learning difficulties

I have worked on many of these projects with children who have learning difficulties. In some instances this has required an adjustment of priorities.

When working with severe learning difficulties I may make many of the musical decisions myself rather than expecting the children to make them. Their achievement may be in the handling and playing of instruments, in working together, in retaining ideas, in responding to each performance. With these children I have particularly enjoyed **Ceremonies**, **Opposites and contrasts**, **The seasons**, and 'Earth', 'Fire' (with frequent emphatic warnings about the dangers of fire and fireworks), and 'Water' from **The elements**.

With groups of children whose learning difficulties are moderate, I have run the projects much as I would with any class of children, ensuring where necessary that the children have adequate adult support when they are working in groups.

LISTENING

Using sounds to create our own music is one way of enjoying and learning to understand music. Listening to other people's music is another. And listening skills are, of course, a vital part of every child's education.

When we roll up our sleeves and work with the actual materials of music, we begin to gain a real insight into what other composers have achieved and how and why they made their musical decisions.

To help you to relate the children's work to that of other composers, I have suggested pieces of music to explore with the class, sometimes before and sometimes after completing a project. I have also taken the liberty of assuming that you may know nothing about the music and have written a guide to exactly what you and the children will be hearing when you listen.

How long should each project take?

The projects will vary greatly in length. Some, e.g., the exploratory games in **The elements**, Project 2 could be completed in one lesson. Others might prove rewarding as extended topic-work spanning a number of lessons and done in conjunction with work in other subjects. Look out for references to cross-curricular work marked ▣

Given time to explore and discover, the children will assemble a repertoire of ideas and techniques that will enable them to deal with music with ever increasing confidence and with a pleasure that will last for a lifetime.

Enjoy the book!

Richard McNicol

9

CHAPTER ONE

Miniatures

THIS CHAPTER IS ABOUT:
Choosing simple sounds
Assembling them to make a short sound-picture.

Bonsai Trees

Netsuke

Model Cat

Think about miniatures.

Sometimes miniatures are made for our convenience. The first computers consisted of rooms full of heavy machinery. Now computers are so small that we all carry pocket calculators.

Sometimes miniaturization is essential because of the kind of job a piece of equipment must do. Think how small the miniature cameras must be that doctors put down patients' throats when they want to look at the inside of their stomachs.

The miniatures in the three pictures were made simply for the pleasure of creating something tiny. How else could we bring a full-grown tree into the house and move it around from one room to another? The bonsai trees in the first picture are only 70cm high and give the *impression* of being full-grown trees. Their branches and roots have been systematically pruned for years to limit their size.

How many branches would a full-sized tree have? And how many leaves?

Both the bonsai trees and the netsuke (pronounced 'netski') carving in the second picture come from Japan where miniatures of all sorts are highly valued. The person who carved the netsuke had to make careful decisions about which details should be left out of the carving in order to make it effective as a miniature.

The cat in the third picture comes from a European gift shop! The person who designed it also decided what to leave in and what to leave out. In fact almost every detail is left out! All that remains are two blobs and a tail. Yet it is perfectly clearly a cat.

Perhaps everybody in the class could make a miniature. They could use modelling clay or even make it out of pottery. Ask the children to reduce detail to an absolute minimum.

PROJECT 1 Owls are calling

Here is a haiku poem by Issa, a Japanese poet who lived from 1763 to 1827.

> *Owls are calling*
> *'come, come'*
> *to the fireflies.*

Haiku poems

Haiku poems give literary expression to the meditation that is an essential element of Zen Buddhism. Haiku is a highly disciplined form and in Japanese only seventeen syllables may be used in a poem. (The translator has managed with a mere ten syllables of English!) Poets strived to produce vivid images with multi-layered meaning, sometimes refining each poem for several years in the quest for perfection.

1 Explain the principle of haiku poems — to capture a perfect picture in a beautiful series of carefully chosen words. Help the class to invent a haiku-style description of something they know well using only eight words.

Here is my attempt to describe playtime:

Children rushing,
football, skipping,
cries of fun,
pain.

2 We know that Issa spent a long time refining his poem. He finally decided that the owls should call 'come, come'. Why did he not write a single 'come' and save himself a word?

▶ I imagine he wanted to imitate the double sound of an owl's call. But perhaps the children have other ideas?

Ask the class to write poems about different animals and birds using no more than eight words.

3 Discuss the idea of inventing a *musical parallel* to Issa's poem. Just as an artist might paint what Issa describes, we will recreate the picture in sound without using any words at all.

Issa is describing a scene at night. What sort of sounds might we use to give an impression of *darkness*? Should they be:
- deep sounds or high sounds?
- quiet sounds or loud sounds?
- long sounds or short sounds?
- fast-moving or slow-moving sounds?

▶ Many people feel that deep, soft sounds are 'dark'. Perhaps also slow-moving sounds. The very low notes of a piano played slowly and randomly, one at a time, with both pedals down (one to sustain the sounds, one to soften them) might fit the bill. But do not impose this idea on the children. What do *they* suggest?

4 Divide the class into groups of five or six to discuss the idea of darkness in sound. When they have decided the sort of things they want to try out, let them choose any instruments they need. Or perhaps they might prefer to use their voices.

Give each group the chance to perform its 'darkness' music and then lead the class in constructive discussion.

▶ You might, for instance, choose one of the quiet pieces and ask the class if they thought it was quiet enough. To illustrate your point, ask the group to play it again *really* quietly and see how much more effective it sounds. Or you might help the children to find the best beaters for the job — soft beaters will produce a less brittle texture.

You might suggest that as an experiment, one group tries its piece again using deeper notes. Do the children find this more effective?

Do be prepared to have some of your ideas rejected. The children may genuinely like their music the way it is and they are, after all, entitled to their opinions!

5 In warm countries like Italy and southern Japan, fireflies can be seen at night as briefly glowing lights, flying for a few metres, then disappearing in the darkness like shooting stars.

What sort of sounds could represent *fireflies* in our musical picture?

▶ If the 'dark' background sounds are deep and quiet it will not be too difficult to find higher, 'brighter' sounds that seem to glow against them — the 'ting' of a triangle, a chime bar or a metallophone, or a couple of notes from a flute, a recorder or a violin.

One sound that seemed particularly effective to me and was suggested by a child, was a mouth-organ.

How many fireflies should we hear? If there are too many the music may sound more like a firework display!

Should the same *sort* of sound be used for *each* firefly (e.g., always a glockenspiel), or should a selection of different 'glowing' sounds be used?

▶ You might help the class to choose sounds by asking one group to play its darkness music whilst a series of volunteers try out glowing instruments against the dark background.

6 When the children have explored some of the available sounds, divide into groups again. The children must:
– choose their firefly sounds
– decide who is going to play them — for example, should one person abandon dark sounds and become a firefly, or should each person briefly stop playing dark sounds, play bright sounds, and then return to dark sounds?

7 All that now remains is to add the *owl* to the musical picture.

▶ Rather than reassemble the class to discuss owl sounds (children are expert owl-hooters!), it might be better to visit each group and suggest that when the fireflies are in place, the children can add *one* owl-call. They must decide whereabouts in their piece it would be most effective to use this one sound.

8 Ask each group to perform to the class.
When Issa wrote his poem he was careful to make it truly miniature. Ask the children to return one last time to their groups and to reduce their music to *twenty seconds* of the most exquisite sound they can produce.

LISTENING

If they don't believe it can be done in twenty seconds, play them the fourth piece from *Five Pieces for Orchestra* op. 10 by Webern! (See **The elements**, Project 2 p. 93, for more details.)

Listen to the opening of *Rain coming* by Toru Takemitsu, which might almost have been inspired by Issa's poem. The first sound we hear, the alto flute (a larger version of the normal concert flute), could be the sound of the owl; the glistening celeste (a metallophone with piano keyboard), the fireflies; the strings, the velvet texture of night.

In fact, *Rain coming* (1982) is more inspired by the French music of Debussy than by any literary model. It does give a clear idea of the delicacy that is so much a part of Japanese art.

Traditional Japanese music is also available in recordings.

PROJECT 2 The butterfly

Here is another haiku by Issa.

> *From burweed*
> *such a butterfly*
> *is born?*

1 Discuss the poem with the class.

Why did Issa make his poem into a question? Did he really think that the butterfly was the child of a patch of weed? Perhaps the chrysalis had been hidden in the weed and when the poet saw the butterfly emerge he was *reminded* of something being born.

Issa may also have been marvelling that two of nature's creations can be so different—a dull tangle of burweed, and a brilliantly coloured butterfly.

> This discussion could lead on to other non-musical work:
> – In *science*, the children might do some work on caterpillars, chrysalises, and butterflies.
> – In *art*, they might paint the event that Issa describes.
> – In *drama*, they could invent a mime or dance of a butterfly emerging from a patch of weed.

The musical version of the poem needs only two ingredients: the shimmering colours of the butterfly's wings, and the tangled uniformity of the burweed.

2 First the *butterfly*.

Sit four volunteers around a metallophone or a large glockenspiel and give each child two soft beaters.

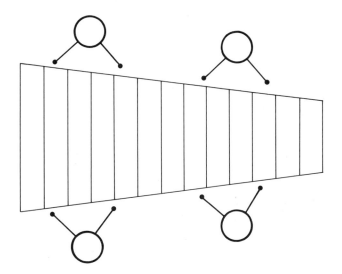

Invite each child to select two notes, then ask the whole group to 'shimmer' as softly as possible, each child alternating his or her two notes (left, right, left, right).

▶ If the texture is to be uniform the four children will need the same sort of beaters. The softness or hardness of these will greatly affect the sound.

This 'shimmering' sound is one of the colours of the butterfly's wings.

3 Can somebody suggest another musical 'colour' that could be 'shimmered' by another group?

▶ The word 'colour' is often used by musicians instead of the word 'timbre'. We say, for example, that the sound of a xylophone (wooden) is a different 'colour' from the sound of a glockenspiel (metal) (though both may be playing the same notes). See also **The elements**, Project 3 p. 94.

Experiment in front of the class with some of the children's suggestions. Four children around a xylophone can produce a 'shimmer' in much the same way as the metallophone group, or try four players 'shimmering' on the softer low notes of recorders.

A mixture of resonant metal instruments (e.g., a triangle or two, a pair of Indian bells, a couple of small chime bars played with metal triangle beaters) might be effective.

▶ It is difficult, however, to produce a colourful 'shimmer' on such instruments as guiros or claves!

4 When the children understand the task clearly, divide into groups of four or five and ask each group to choose instruments and to produce quickly a delicate 'shimmer'.

▶ The 'shimmers' will almost certainly sound more delicate if each group chooses one *sort* of instrument, e.g., a group of metal instruments, a group of blown instruments, etc. It is harder to achieve a blend of sound on disparate instruments.

When the 'shimmers' are ready, bring the class back together and sit the groups in a circle on the floor. Each group will represent a different 'colour' of the butterfly.

5 Explain that group 1 is to start playing as softly as possible and can then get a little louder.

After a few seconds group 2 can begin to play, *so softly that it is at first imperceptible.* Then it too can become a shade louder.

As group 1 becomes aware of group 2, it slowly dies away and stops, leaving group 2 playing alone. Then group 3 starts from nothing, and so on.

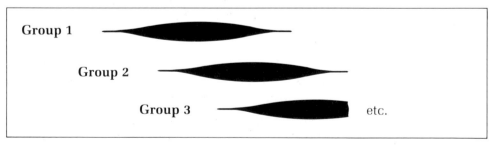

No join should ever be heard!

6 Practise this gradual changing of colour until the children can do it really efficiently. If a group simply cannot play softly enough to get in *unnoticed* (recorders for example will find this difficult), the preceding group should get correspondingly louder to help them.

► Encourage the children to play *really* softly where possible. No player, child or professional, ever truly plays as softly as possible until asked to!

Would the 'colour changing' be easier or more effective if the groups played in a different order?

7 Now turn the children's attention to the *burweed*.
The weed is thickly tangled and uniform in colour. If we use too bright a sound to portray it, we may detract from the impact of the butterfly.
Could the children *use their voices* to invent a dull tangle of sound?

► In the previous project we discussed the concept of deep sounds as dark sounds. Deep sounds can also be considered dull and unobtrusive.

As a class activity ask the children to murmur very softly at the bottom of their voices. Ask them to try humming with lips closed, then to try muttering random words. Which do they think sounds more tangled?

8 Appoint someone to stand in front of the class and be a conductor. When the conductor points at an individual in the class, that person's voice should become slightly louder than the rest, then subside again into the 'tangle'.
Let two or three different children in turn have a go at being the conductor. Can they make the 'tangles' come and go all over the class-room?

9 Now ask the children to go back into their ring of colour groups. Stand a conductor in the middle.
Start the burweed music. Then when group 1 decides it is time, the butterfly begins to emerge, colour by colour.

10 When the children have tried the piece once, ask them to make some decisions:
– Should the burweed sound continue as the butterfly emerges, or should it stop at some earlier point?
– When each colour group has performed should the piece simply end or can the class think of some way of creating a climax to the piece?

► When the last group has entered, for example, all the groups might join in for a brief louder section.

– Could the class choose one magical sound to bring the piece to an end?

► It is not difficult to imagine the glowing 'ting' of a pair of Indian bells echoing on at the end of the piece. But of course the children must decide what *they* want.

Finally, if the children are enjoying performing the piece, it will almost certainly go on much too long! Remind them that all of this must take place in just thirty seconds.

PROJECT 3 **At prayer**

*At prayer,
bead-swinging
at mosquitos.*

This poem seems to indicate that Issa had a sense of humour — or does it? I wonder if he might have felt that praying was like trying to hit a mosquito with a string of beads. But it *might* be a simple description of monks trying to pray in peace in a mosquito-ridden temple.

These are only two of the many layers of meaning that are contained in a haiku.

1 Discuss *praying* with the class.

Different people and different religions pray in different ways.

Buddhist priests at prayer

Christians praying

Moslems praying

Some people pray silently, others speak out loud. Some kneel, some stand, some prostrate themselves. Perhaps several religions are represented in your school. Could children describe the ritual of their own religion?

This project may of course grow naturally out of, or into, work about different religions and beliefs.

2 In many religions prayer is *chanted*. Many words are intoned on one note, a change of note often signifying the end of a phrase or sentence:

```
 •    •    •    •    •    •    •    •
                                        •
We  are  thankful  for  the  food  we  eat.
```

Chanting is not exclusively a religious activity. Warriors may chant to prepare themselves for battle. Football fans chant in support of their team. We could even chant the class register, the lunch menu or the highway code!

In some chants people *echo* phrases sung by their priest or leader.

Chant a short sentence to the class using the lower register of your voice. Chant all the words on one note except the last one. Drop this to a lower note — it doesn't matter which.

Can the children chant or echo the sentence back to you? This is called 'call and response'.

Chant another sentence, this time altering the note for a word or two in the middle of the sentence as well.

3 Will one of the children volunteer to take over your job as chant leader? Let several children in turn have a go at leading.

Of course, chanting is not the only form of religious music. Hymns are important in some western religions. Can any of the children tell you about any other forms of religious music?

4 Divide the class into groups of six and ask each group to invent some sort of religious music.

▶ Move between the groups to see how their ideas are developing. Some groups may decide to invent their own unique sort of music, perhaps like something they have seen on television. I have seen tribal 're- ligious ceremonies' of extremely dubious authenticity in Tarzan films, for instance! If there is strong resistance to using voices, suggest that they first clap their calls and responses. Then they can move on to vocal sounds, perhaps making up their own language.

Ask each group to perform its prayer music to the class.

5 Buddhist monks, like Roman Catholics, use strings of beads as an aid to meditation and prayer. High-powered business executives sometimes use similar aids to stave off stress!

How might the 'clicking of beads' be represented in our music?

▶ Claves (note the correct way of holding them),

castanets, wood blocks, or indeed anything wooden might be used for the sound of clicking beads.

Discuss and explore the possibilities. Can any objects be found in the class that would serve this purpose?

6 Ask the groups to add some bead-clicking to their prayer music. They will need to decide:
– whether the clicking should be continuous or intermittent?
– whether it should be regular or irregular in rhythm?
– whether one sound should be used (e.g., claves) or a variety of sounds?

▶ If the children click too often it may sound more like a group of woodpeckers than a group of priests! Encourage them to use their bead sounds sparingly.

7 The last element in the poem is the *mosquitos*. Why are the monks 'bead-swinging at mosquitos'?

▶ You may wish to explain that the monks will only be trying to frighten the mosquitos away, not to kill them. Buddhists believe in reincarnation and all life is, therefore, sacred. If you killed a mosquito you wouldn't know who you might be killing!

Can anyone suggest a sound for mosquitos?

▶ Here, a violin played close to the bridge with a trembling bow might be the perfect sound.

Anyone can do it — you don't have to be a violinist.

Comb and paper, and some of the sounds on an electric keyboard might be similarly effective. What ideas can the children suggest?

8 Discuss the assembling of the complete piece.
 – how much mosquito sound should we hear?
 – how should the beads and the mosquitos interact?
 – could there be one climactic moment to give shape to each piece?
 – would it be a good idea to tie the whole piece together with continuous prayer music?

9 Send the children back into their groups and visit each group as work progresses. Make sure that the children use only the three elements we have discussed. It is quite unnecessary to introduce anything else.

► Additional ideas will only make the task more complex (and the results perhaps less satisfactory). Assembling limited materials effectively is one of the fundamental skills of composing.

10 Invite each group to perform its completed work to the class.

LISTENING

As a complement to this project the children could listen to some religious chanting.

Gregorian chant, the European Christian chant of the Middle Ages (still sung today in Roman Catholic ritual), and the similar *Russian Orthodox chant* are readily available on record.

You might also explore recordings on the French 'Harmonia Mundi' label, including the simple but fascinating chanting of *Tibetan monks* of the *Bon* religion which pre-dates Buddhism.

PROJECT 4 Dawn chorus

1 Launch this project by listening to some *birdsong* with the class.

Perhaps you could all go outside and listen to some birds singing. You might even be able to capture their songs on tape with a cassette recorder.

If this is not possible you could use a recording of birdsong. Records of birdsong can be bought at major record stores, or your local Resources Centre may be able to help you.

2 Discuss birdsong:
- do birds sing in long or short bursts?
- do they endlessly invent new music or do they repeat themselves?
- do their songs contain many different notes or do they use a small range of notes?

Birdsong

Birdsongs do of course vary, but most birds limit themselves to a small repertoire of musical shapes. The *cuckoo* is an extreme example — it uses only two notes and one unchanging rhythm.

We might write the cuckoo's song like this:

Two short notes of equal length, the second lower than the first.

Write the cuckoo's song on the board. Can the children deduce which bird it is? Perhaps someone could come out and play it on a xylophone.

3 Now write this *imaginary* birdsong on the board:

Can somebody perform it and then explain why they played what they did?

▶ Each shape consists of two short notes (the second higher than the first), followed by a longer note which is lower than the others. From my graphic there is no way of deducing exactly which notes should be used or how wide to make the gaps. But as birds generally use a narrow range of notes the sounds will be fairly close together.

We might represent it on the glockenspiel using the notes:

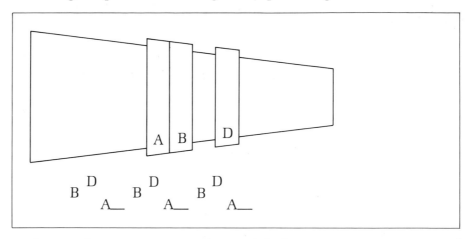

The 'graphic notation' using dots and dashes is my own invention and is in no way definitive. You might like to devise your own different method.

4 Our bird now adds a new musical shape to the end of its song:

Will someone come out and play the complete song?

▶ The additional six notes are of course higher in pitch than the others. I have written them in line, in an attempt to indicate that they are repetitions of the *same* note. Also they are closer together to indicate that they take less time to play (i.e., they are quicker). You might play them on E on the glockenspiel:

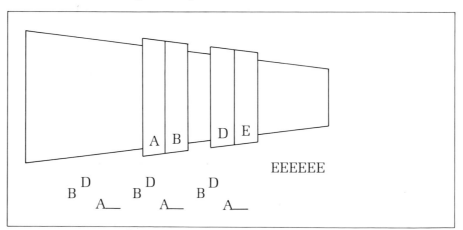

5 Ask each child to choose a partner.

Can each pair of children invent a short birdsong using *only two* different shapes? If they decide to use an instrument they must choose four notes and use only these for their birdsong.

▶ I have suggested that the children work in pairs so that they can discuss ideas and support one another. Perhaps they should take one shape each and perform the birdsong between them. If they decide to use an instrument like a glockenspiel I would take off all bars except those chosen, for example A, B, D, and E. Player one can then invent a shape using only A and B, and player two an answering shape using D and E.

Perform each birdsong.

Can anyone devise a way of writing down their birdsong for someone else to perform?

6 Finish the project by helping the class to create a *dawn chorus*.

66 *If you get up really early in spring or summer, just as the sun is rising, you may be lucky enough to hear the first bird start to sing. Soon another will wake and answer, and before you know it, the whole world seems to erupt into birdsong. This is the dawn chorus. Then as the sun gathers strength, the birdsong dies away.* 99

Ask the class to decide:
– which pair of children should be the first bird to sing
– how soon the second bird should answer
– whether or not another pair of birds should call and answer before the full dawn chorus begins
– how quickly the other birds should join in
– how the dawn chorus should end.

7 Perform the dawn chorus.

When it is in full swing it will sound very busy indeed. Can the children perform it *without anyone saying a word*? The sound of voices will almost certainly spoil the effect.

If possible, record the performance so that the children can listen to it and discuss it afterwards. They will have been so busy playing that amid all the confusion of sound they may not have got a clear idea of what the piece sounds like to a listener.

LISTENING

The French composer Olivier Messiaen (born 1908), has had a life-long passion for birdsong. It abounds in his music, 'collected' by the composer himself from all over the world and is transformed into a unique stylized musical language.

Listen to *Oiseaux Exotiques* (1956) in which the solo piano plays great blocks of birdsong. Although this piano-birdsong is written in chords, whereas a bird sings only one note at a time, the principle of short, repeated shapes can be clearly heard and the music is unmistakably birdsong.

In the score Messiaen writes the name of each bird over its song.

Oiseaux Exotiques opens with slow ceremonial music followed immediately by the first block of piano birdsong. This in turn is followed by a dawn chorus played on piccolo (lesser green Malaysian leaf-bird), flute, oboe, and two clarinets (Baltimore oriole), glockenspiel (red-billed mesia from China), xylophone (California thrasher, a wood-thrush).

I have found that children are often amazed how similar Messiaen's dawn chorus is to theirs, but they usually feel that their music was better!

PROJECT 5 The nightingale

*Nightingale's song
this morning
soaked with rain.*

1 Read Issa's poem to the class.

The *nightingale* does not limit itself to one or two shapes of music. It is one of the world's most virtuosic birds.

It does not, however, keep on inventing *new* shapes — it sings a repertoire of several fragments which it places in different orders.

Here is my impression of the sort of structure a nightingale might sing, using six different shapes:

1 2 3 1 4 1 5   2 3 1 6   4 1 5 3 2 1

▶ This is a totally unscientific structure and birdlovers may take me to task accordingly! But it does illustrate a principle of construction.

Introduce this idea to the class by writing the above nightingale pattern on the board and inviting three pairs of songsters from Project 4 to bring their instruments to the front of the class.

Number the children one to six. Can they now play the nightingale's song?

2 Divide the whole class into groups of three pairs and ask each group to devise its *own* nightingale song, using only the shapes that were invented in Project 4.

Remind the children that players must never overlap — it is only *one* nightingale singing in each group.

3 Issa talks about a morning 'soaked with rain'.

If we wanted to create a musical impression of *rain*, would we need:
– few or many notes?
– long notes or short notes?
– high notes or deep notes?
– loud notes or soft notes?
– a variety of sounds or lots of the same?

▶ One solution to this problem is for as many children as possible to take one chime bar and one beater. The rain starts with children playing very softly and only very occasionally, at random. As the rain intensifies, people play more often (but still quietly). The same principle can be applied using fingers drumming on desk-tops.

What other ideas can the children suggest?

Help the class to invent a rain piece that starts gradually, increases to a downpour, then eases and stops.

4 Nightingales sing at night. But the poem says 'this morning'. Could the poet mean at *daybreak*?

Ask the class to suggest a sound to represent the *rising sun*.

▶ The warm glow of a suspended cymbal played quietly with two soft beaters occurs to me, but I expect the children will have a better idea!

5 Now ask each group to assemble its own version of the poem.

▶ Here a problem may arise. When the whole class made a rain piece, it took many hands to make it sound realistic. A group of six children may only be able to give a symbolic hint of rain.

Point out to the children that this is exactly what *miniatures* do. Remind them of the miniature cat pictured at the beginning of this chapter. It too is just a 'hint' of a cat!

Each group must decide for itself:
– where the rising sun should come
– when the hint of rain is to be heard
– how long and how often the nightingale should sing
– how the piece should end.
And the piece should be no longer than thirty seconds!

LISTENING

To hear a real nightingale singing in a musical context, listen to 'The Pines of Gianicolo,' third movement of *The Pines of Rome* by Respighi.

At the very end of this magical movement, the composer asks that the orchestra play very quietly whilst a gramophone record of a nightingale singing is played through loudspeakers.

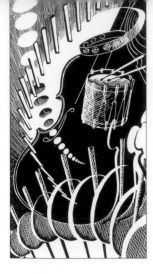

CHAPTER TWO

Pulse and rhythm

THIS CHAPTER IS ABOUT:

Discovering pulse

Inventing rhythms and fitting them together

Writing down simple rhythmic pieces.

Pulse

Inside each of us is a *pulse*, a ticking clock that measures the seconds, the hours, and the years away—our heart. Sometimes it beats faster, sometimes slower, but it never stops.

Perhaps because pulse is fundamental to life, it is also fundamental to music. Music does exist, of course, that has no pulse; in particular, some of the music of our own time. But the vast bulk of music invented over the centuries lives and is carried forward by pulse.

PROJECT 1 Finding a pulse

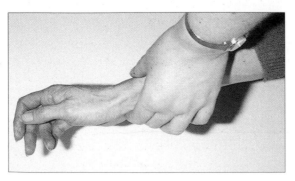

1 Think about pulse.

Can the children find their own pulse? It will be easier to find if they place their *fingers*, not thumbs, on their wrists. Or perhaps the side of the neck is a better place, just under the chin.

When everyone has found their pulse ask them to count silently how many times their heart pulses in thirty seconds. You can be the time-keeper! Ask each child to write down the number of times his or her heart beats in one minute, i.e., their pulse-rate.

▶ If you can borrow a metronome, it is fun to show the class how fast a particular child's heart is beating. If, for instance, Mandy Smith tells you that her heart beats eighty-four times in a minute, set the metronome at eighty-four and let the whole class listen to the speed of Mandy's heart. Metronomes give beats per minute, which is the standard way composers record on paper the speed at which they would like their music to go.

2 Find your own pulse and tap its speed out on your desk. Ask the children to find their own pulse again. Call out somebody's name. Can that person tap the speed of his or her pulse on the table-top? What about somebody else?

Could two people tap their different pulses simultaneously without one altering speed to match the other? This is quite difficult; perhaps even impossible!

3 Explain to the children that music too has a 'heartbeat' — a pulse that keeps it alive in just the same way as our heart keeps us alive. And we can find the pulse of a piece of music just as we can find our own pulse. Of course, we can't put our fingers on a piece of music's wrist, but we can *listen* for its pulse. We may not even need to listen very hard; our foot may do the job for us. For when we tap our feet in time to a piece of music, it is the pulse of the music that we are tapping.

Listen to some music with the class. You may choose a lively piece of pop music, or you may choose a 'classical' piece, e.g.:
– *The Liberty Bell* by Souza (or any other march)
– *Country Gardens* by Percy Grainger
– the opening of *Eine Kleine Nachtmusik* by Mozart
– the first movement of 'Spring' from *The Four Seasons* by Vivaldi.
Or you may decide to sing a song:

There	was	an	old	lady	who	swallowed	a	fly	
	●			●		●		●	(pulse)

▶ Choose a brisk, foot-tapping piece of music for your first exploration of pulse. In some slower, more thoughtful music, the pulse can vary in speed and may be quite hard to discern.

4 Ask the class to listen to the music first. Then very quietly, with just two fingers on the palm of the hand, to clap the pulse.

Now stop the music. Get one half of the class to continue clapping the pulse with you. Can the other half clap *two* pulses to each *one* of yours?

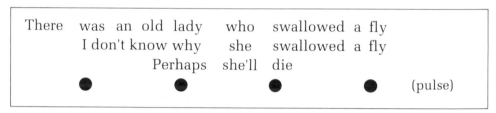

5 One more game. Sing 'There was an old lady' with the children and ask them to clap the pulse as they sing. I expect you will put one clap into the space before 'Perhaps', and one clap into the space at the end, before starting the next verse.

There	was	an	old	lady	who	swallowed	a fly
	I don't	know	why		she	swallowed	a fly
			Perhaps	she'll	die		
●			●		●		● (pulse)

Sing the verse again and this time ask the children to put *two* claps into each of the spaces (making the spaces twice as long).

Then try three claps.

It might be fun to sing the whole song adding an extra clap in the spaces for each new verse.

PROJECT 2 Name-chants

1 Imagine that Mandy Smith is running in the Olympic Games.

> ▶ (Mandy is an imaginary member of my class; you can choose the name of one of the children in your class!)

The whole class has gone to watch her and they desperately want her to win. As the last lap begins she is just in the lead.

Get the class to *chant* her name to drive her on to win. Can they also clap the *pulse* that underlies the *rhythm* of their chant?

> ▶ Whereas *pulse* is the regular foot-tapping beat that underlies music or a chant, *rhythm* is the sometimes irregular series of long and short sounds that make up words, melodies, and of course, Mandy Smith's name. I expect my class would chant:

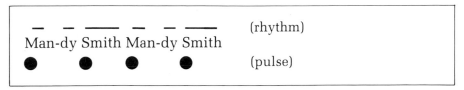

2 Terry Robinson is running in the same race. He too has his fans and they would much rather he won!

Ask the class to clap the same speed of pulse as for Mandy Smith but this time to chant for Terry Robinson.

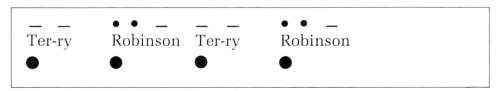

3 Now is the time to take the class to the other side of the playground, as far away from the other classrooms as possible! Divide the class in half and, with everyone clapping the pulse, get one half of the class to chant for Mandy and the other half for Terry.

Man-dy	Smith	Man-dy	Smith
Ter - ry	Robinson	Ter - ry	Robinson

Ann McCormack is coming up fast in the outside lane!

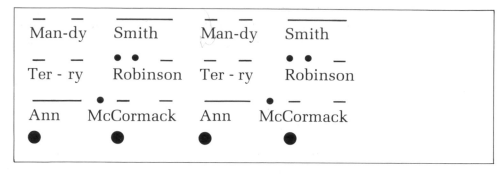

4 Divide the class into groups of five or six and ask each group to use its members' names to invent its own Olympic name-chant. Or perhaps they would prefer to use the names of more famous athletes.

Give each group a chance to perform to the class.

5 Could all the groups perform together to make one enormous chant?

PROJECT 3 Instrumental name-chants

▶ If Project 2 has been enjoyable and productive, try extending it by using instruments in place of voices.

1 Begin by asking each group in turn to perform its piece from Project 2, *clapping* the name-rhythms instead of chanting them. You might take over the role of pulse player, perhaps using a pair of claves or a tambourine so that your pulse doesn't get mixed up with their clapped rhythms. Then see if the groups can clap their pieces without anyone keeping the pulse.

2 Now move on to the idea of performing the pieces on instruments instead of voices. The instruments each group chooses will make a great deal of difference to the effectiveness of the music.

As an example, ask one group to try its piece using a group of disparate sounding instruments:

large drum, one note on a recorder, claves, large cymbal, Indian bells, maraca would be a suitably improbable combination.

Then for comparison perform the same piece using only *wooden* instruments:

> claves (possibly two pairs of different sizes), wood block, a chime bar beater on a tabletop, castanets, a maraca held in one hand and struck with the other.

3 What do the children think are the drawbacks and the advantages of each group of instruments?

> ► There will almost certainly have been a difficulty of balance (the relative loudness of different instruments) in the performance using the first group of instruments. The large cymbal probably drowned out all the rest, except possibly the large drum. The balance with the second group should have been much clearer, with every instrument audible.
>
> Here are some other combinations that I think would be effective:
> – all small metal instruments
> – all small wooden instruments
> – a mixture of small metal and wooden instruments, e.g., indian bell, claves, wood block, small triangle, guiro, maraca

> – string instruments (violin, cello, guitar, autoharp) plucked
> – different sizes of drum and tambourine, perhaps played with a cloth or a finger on the skin to deaden the sound.

4 Help the children to choose instruments for their groups and to practise this new version of their pieces.

The project could finish with each group performing a 'sandwich' piece:

> chant version, instrumental version, chant version.

PROJECT 4 Peter Piper

Peter Piper picked a peck of pickled pepper.
Where's the peck of pickled pepper Peter Piper picked?

Tongue-twisters

The challenge of the tongue-twister is to say it in a steady stream of sounds without stumbling or disturbing the pulse. It may be fun to perform but it is rather uninteresting to listen to! Its rhythm never changes: four even-length sounds to every pulse.

---

1 Write 'Peter Piper' up on the board. Then take the class through it clapping the pulse for them. Perhaps at first give a pulse clap on each word (except, of course, 'a', 'of', and 'the') at a nice steady pace (marked ● below). Then as the children get better at it, a pulse every other word (again excluding 'a', 'of', and 'the'):

Peter	Piper	picked a peck of pickled pepper
●		● ●

2 We could vary the rhythm of the tongue-twister and make it much more interesting for the listener if we left out some of the words. Let's try missing out *every* word except 'Peter Piper' and 'pickled pepper'. Give the class two claps in and see how they get on.

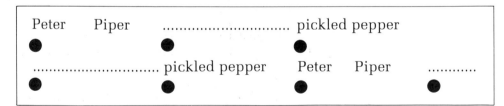

Chant the phrase several times continuously to give everyone a chance to get into the swing of it.

► If the children find it difficult to leave the gaps (I do!), get them to whisper the complete verse, saying only the relevant words aloud as they get to them.

3 How would it sound if the class divided up into two groups; group 1 saying 'Peter Piper' and 'pickled pepper' and group 2 only the word 'picked' — but very loudly!

group 1   Peter   Piper .... pickled pepper
group 2   .... PICKED...................................
　　　　●　　　　　　　●　　　　　　　●

group 1   .... pickled pepper Peter Piper ....
group 2   ....PICKED
　　　　●　　　　　●　　　　　●　　　　　●

Can anyone suggest another layer that could be added?

4 A group of children saying the word that comes on each pulse might form the next layer.

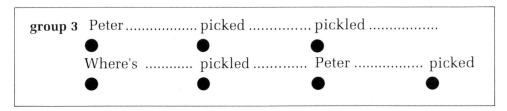

These regularly spaced words might help to hold the whole piece together. Children who find the exercise easy might find this layer more challenging:

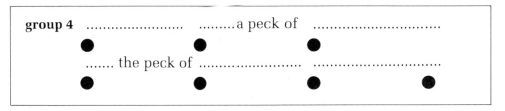

5 When the class understands the game clearly, divide into groups of four or five and ask each group to invent its own layered version of 'Peter Piper'.

▶ Here it might be wise to take the precaution of eavesdropping on each group to make sure that no one is out of his or her depth. A child who is struggling might be given the important task of saying the very first 'Peter' to get the piece off to a good start.

6 After each group has performed its piece to the class, discuss ways of *extending* the pieces to make them a little more substantial.

The easiest way of extending any piece of music is simply to *repeat* all or part of it. Composers do this all the time. But let's try something a little more sophisticated. Suppose one performer starts, all alone. On the first repetition another member of the group joins in.

Would one of the groups volunteer to show the class how this would sound if the process were continued?

7 To finish the piece, everyone could simply stop when one member of the group gives a signal. But there are many other ways of bringing a piece to a satisfactory conclusion. Here are a few of the possibilities:
- reverse the opening build-up so that the person who started alone finishes alone
- drop out in reverse order, so that the child who started the piece drops out first and the last one in finishes alone
- get softer and softer until the music fades away
- get louder and louder, and finish with a bang
- get slower and stop
- start missing out notes until there are none left.

8 What do the children prefer? Give each group the chance to develop its piece and perform it to the class.

LISTENING

The American composer Steve Reich constructs his music in a very similar way to some of the projects in this chapter. He loves to invent the sort of interlocking rhythms that we found using 'Peter Piper'.

Reich repeats rhythms over and over again until we are almost lulled to sleep. Then he will catch our attention with a tiny alteration in the rhythm or the notes, and off go the repetitions again.

His music has strong jazz roots and makes wonderful, high-quality 'easy listening'.

Play the beginning of *Drumming* to the class. As in 'Peter Piper' the four players build up interlocking rhythms using drums and repeat them over and over again. Although it is not done in quite the same way as 'Peter Piper', the principle of the music is the same.

Drumming is an extremely long piece of music. Be careful not to allow it to outstay its welcome with the children.

Try using it for three or four listening sessions. If you jump forward you will easily identify new sections sounding like:
- bass xylophones (actually played on marimbas)
- metallophones (vibraphones)
- glockenspiels (glockenspiels)
- xylophones (xylophones).

Point out to the children how secretively new rhythms find their way into music that *seems* to go on without changing.

PROJECT 5 Exchanging notes

▶ The pieces in Project 4 can equally well be performed on percussion instruments. The words are merely a way of arriving at interesting rhythms. If Project 4 has proved worthwhile and the children are still enthusiastic, you might like to take it a stage further.

1 Sit one of the 'Peter Piper' groups round a xylophone, a glockenspiel or a metallophone, and give each child a beater.

First ask the group to perform its spoken version of 'Peter Piper' from Project 4, to make sure that the children haven't forgotten it. Then ask player 1 to choose a note and *play* his or her line of the piece at the same time as saying the syllables (using only this one note).

2 As player 1 keeps repeating the line, ask player 2 to choose another note and join in playing the second strand of the piece.

Player 2 might wish to try out two or three different notes before deciding which one goes best with the first player's note.

Now player 3 can join in, in the same way, then players 4 and 5.

▶ Let each player make his or her own decision which note to play. We adults may find some of the choices strange but it is important that the children gain confidence in their own musical decisions and it is, after all, a matter of opinion.

3 When the group can perform the piece confidently in this way, ask the children to stop saying the syllables and to perform the piece using only the notes.

4 Now a development of the game. When the whole group is playing, player 1 changes to a different note. After a while player 2 does the same, and so on until everyone has changed note.

Then the process is reversed and everyone finds their way back to the note they started on.

Finally, the children must devise a way of finishing their piece.

5 The rest of the class can play a *listening game* while the group performs. Ask the children to listen with eyes closed. When it comes to the point where the performers change notes, challenge the listening children to put their hands up every time they hear a change of note. Then put them down again and wait for the next change.

6 If you have enough instruments, divide into groups so that everyone has a chance to take part in an exchanging-note piece. If not, perhaps other groups can have their chance at another time of the day.

7 This project can sometimes produce beautiful pieces of music. And occasionally, by good luck, the different groups can be juxtaposed and even superimposed with considerable success.

> ▶ The fun of inventing music is quite simply in *messing about with sounds*, trying first one thing and then another. This is what composers have done since time immemorial. If they discover something they like, they use it; if they don't like it, they try something else.

If the class has made up four or five note-changing pieces, take a little time to experiment.

This time *you* direct the experiments. Try groups 1 and 2 simultaneously. They may have to adjust their speeds so that they fit together.

What do the children think of it?

No good? Never mind, it doesn't matter and it was worth a try!

Now groups 3 and 4 together. How was that?

> ▶ If things obviously don't work, don't be afraid to abandon them. But don't give up *too* easily either. If the children are still with you and are still enjoying the lesson, keep experimenting. In this way some of the most lovely surprises occur!

LISTENING

Octet, another piece written by Steve Reich for himself and seven friends to play, makes excellent complementary listening to this project.

Play the *listening game* with Reich's music. His phrases repeat almost endlessly and change comes so gradually as to be almost imperceptible.

Ask the children to indicate to you each time they hear a change take place in *Octet*.

PROJECT 6 Music on paper — exchanging ideas

1 Write 'Peter Piper' up on the board separating out each syllable:
Pe-ter Pi-per picked a peck of pick-led pep-per
Would one of the children like to come up and underline the words he or she used in the 'Peter Piper' piece?
e.g. <u>Pe-ter</u> <u>Pi-per</u> picked a peck of <u>pick-led</u> <u>pep-per</u>

2 Take a wood block or a pair of claves. Would a volunteer play a note on each of the underlined syllables while the class quietly chants the complete tongue-twister?

Would another child come up and add another layer underneath the first one?

▶ At this stage it is helpful to draw a grid on the board so that each sound and each silence has its own square. Extend this grid as you add new layers.

Pe-	ter	Pi-	per					pick-	led	pep-	per
				picked	a						

Now choose an instrument so that the second layer can be added to the first.

▶ You might try performing the two layers *without* the class reciting the words. Perhaps you should lightly clap the pulse to give the two performers a little support.

Add another layer, and another.

▶ If all is going well, the interlocking rhythms of the four layers may now make even the clapped pulse unnecessary. But if the children find the task difficult, keep the class quietly reciting the rhyme throughout. The important thing is that the exercise works and the children succeed!

3 Take a rest from 'Peter Piper'. Draw an empty grid and invite a child to fill in some of the spaces, leaving others empty. The child might decide on:

Can someone else perform what has been written?

4 When the class has got the hang of this way of writing music down, return to 'Peter Piper'. Divide the children into their groups and ask them to write down their 'Peter Piper' pieces using *dots* in place of the syllables or words. They should indicate clearly at the beginning of each line of the grid the instrument to be used.

Player 1: claves	●	●	●	●	
Player 2: Indian bell					●
Player 3: wood block	●				●
Player 4: triangle					

Now ask each group to exchange its paper with another group. Can the groups practise and perform their friends' pieces?

5 So far we have notated every sound with a dot. If we could invent a series of more elaborate signs we could notate our pieces more precisely.

Give the class an example—a scrape on a guiro lasting two syllables could be written:

What ideas do the children have for developing a more expressive form of notation?

▶ CAUTION: beware of being led into notation for 'tuned' instruments, i.e., those that play several different notes—xylophones, recorders, etc. That would raise more complex issues and is better saved for another occasion.

For the moment, stick to instruments that play one note. The parameters that then arise are:
- length of sound
- loudness or softness of sound
- quality of sound.

▶ Here are a few possibilities:

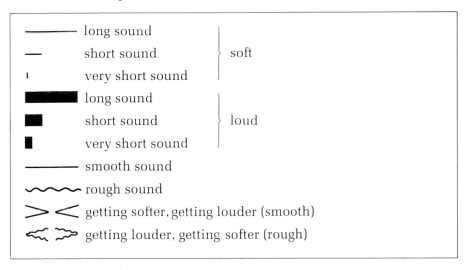

▶ N.B. These signs are not 'official' — I have just invented them!

6 Return the notated 'Peter Piper' pieces to their original groups. Would the children like to revise their writing down of the pieces using new signs to indicate such things as loudness and softness, length of notes, and quality of sound? They must remember to put a *key* to the signs at the end of their pieces or nobody will know what the signs mean!

Notation

Music is notated so that someone else at some other time can perform your music without you having to be there to tell them how to do it. The vast bulk of the world's music is *not* notated. Some is remembered and passed on to other performers and even other generations; some is invented spontaneously (improvised) and then forgotten. Notation is largely a Western phenomenon.

CHAPTER THREE

Opposites and contrasts

THIS CHAPTER IS ABOUT:

Loud sounds and soft sounds
Short sounds and long sounds
Rough sounds and smooth sounds
High sounds and deep sounds
Musical structure.

One of the most useful inventing skills we can learn in music is how to make effective use of the simplest of musical material. The aim of these projects is to help the children to use simple pairs of opposites and contrasts to invent elegantly constructed miniature pieces of music.

Think about opposites and contrasts.

Ask the children to make a list of *opposites*.

How many of them were true opposites? Right and left and up and down clearly are. Boy and girl are not. When we talk about opposites, we often mean *contrasts*.

Ask the children to work in pairs or small groups to produce a short performance that features opposites or contrasts. They might decide to act out a short scene, to dance or mime, or they might decide to produce some sounds, musical or otherwise.

When the work is completed, ask each pair or group to perform to the class.

This exploration of opposites and contrasts might lead into other areas of the curriculum. In *painting*, children could investigate bright colours and dark colours, and in *drawing*, they could contrast shapes with rounded lines and shapes with straight lines. The children might write *poems* that contrast images of stillness with images of great activity or even violence. A sensitive exploration of some of the work of the First World War poets, with their juxtaposition of pastoral stillness and savage destruction, might lead to discussion of more contemporary issues—nuclear arms, violence on television, the threat man poses to the environment.

PROJECT 1 Loud sounds and soft sounds

1 You might launch this project as a *game* at the end of the day. Take a piece of paper and explain to the class that it is a musical instrument which you can play in a number of different ways. But today you are only going to rustle it.

Ask for a helper and offer him or her the use of a shoe and the top of your table. Your instrument is always *soft*, your friend's is always *loud*!

The rules of the piece you are going to perform to the class are extremely simple. Whisper them to your helper. You will rustle your paper *until* the shoe is banged on the table. The bang will stop you, but after a short pause you will start again. Only when your helper bangs *twice* will you finally stop rustling the paper.

Perform the piece to the class. Can the children work out what the rules were? If not, perform it again.

Can anyone suggest a new set of rules for a different performance of the loud-soft piece? If someone can, invite them to come and play it with you.

2 When everyone understands the principle involved—of responding to a musical signal—ask each child to choose a partner. Each pair must decide on two contrasting 'instruments', one loud and one soft, to bring from home the next day. Their task will be to invent an 'opposites piece' that will hold the interest of the class for thirty to forty seconds.

Next morning, give the children a little time to prepare and practise their pieces. Some may well have been prepared on the telephone the night before!

▶ CAUTION. Children's minds are dangerously fertile! Remind the class that the aim of the project is to invent a *short* piece (forty seconds at most), using *only* the two contrasting sounds.

43

3 Ask each pair to perform to the class and lead the class in constructive discussion of the effectiveness of each piece (see Introduction p. 8).

4 Here are three loud/soft pieces which I personally feel would be effective. I have invented a way of writing them down.

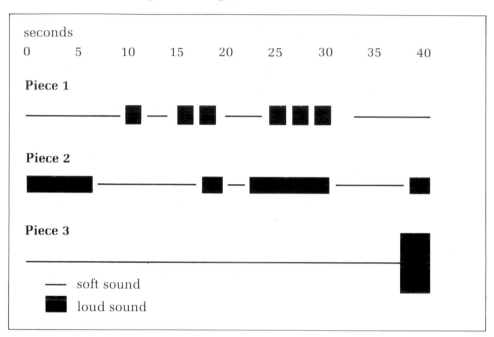

Each piece is carefully structured, the first with a logical progression from one loud sound to three loud sounds and a fragment of soft sound to round it off. The second is almost symmetrical, while the third is designed to shock — a long, continuous soft sound to induce a feeling of security, then a mighty crash! Choose suitable instruments for each and try them out.

LISTENING

When Mussorgsky decided to include a 'picture' of ancient Roman subterranean burial chambers in *Pictures at an Exhibition*, he too invented a piece of music that relies entirely on the effect of loud sounds contrasted suddenly with soft sounds.

'Catacombs' (No. 8 of the *Pictures*), benefited hugely from Ravel's decision to arrange Mussorgsky's piano original for symphony orchestra, and it is in Ravel's version that the piece is now normally performed.

After playing the piece to the children you might like to point out to them:
– the constant alternation of loud and soft .
– that the music is never allowed to become predictable (for we, the listeners, are intended to be in those catacombs experiencing the horror of seeing each new body)

- how a section of trumpet melody is introduced just as we are beginning to get used to the idea of loud and soft chords
- how skilfully the ending is contrived, leaving us hanging in mid-air wondering what to expect next
- how *short* the piece is—Mussorgsky was well aware that tension cannot be sustained forever.

When I listen to 'Catacombs', I feel that Mussorgsky was trying to achieve a number of things:
- the echoes you might hear in catacombs
- the dark dignity of the place
- the sadness and awe that surrounds death
- the sense of horror that I mentioned above.

What do the children hear in this music? How does it make *them* feel?

Can my observations about the effectiveness of Mussorgsky's music be applied to the children's pieces? Do they:
- avoid becoming too predictable?
- contain sufficient variety?
- end well?
- stop before we become bored with them?
- achieve the atmosphere or effect the children wanted?

We must not forget, of course, that Mussorgsky and Ravel were both professional composers at the highest level!

PROJECT 2 Short sounds and long sounds

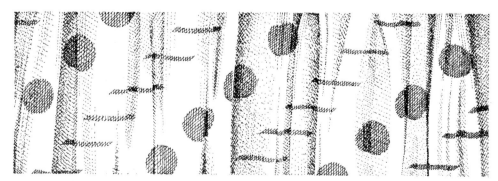

1 Imagine that the class has been asked to design some curtains for the classroom. The pattern on the curtains must be made up entirely of brush strokes in one colour and dots in another. These must not be random—the school governors have insisted on something orderly!

Discuss different ways of organizing strokes and dots to make a design. We might alternate blocks of strokes and blocks of dots, perhaps to make up a series of bold squares. We might have a splash of strokes in the middle of each curtain surrounded by a texture of dots. Ask the children to suggest some other possibilities.

Ask each child to paint a design for the curtains. Display the designs on the wall and ask the governors to come and see them!

2 Now turn the attention of the class to sounds.

In just the same way as we can make contrasting brush marks (long brush strokes, short brush dots), we can also make contrasting sounds — *long* sounds and *short* sounds.

Take long sounds first. Our voices can produce long sounds. Which instruments are suitable for long sounds?

▶ Keyboards, recorders, violins are obvious candidates. Metallophones resonate for quite a long time. A triangle can be rung continuously.

A long sound can be made to do all sorts of interesting things. It can start softly and get gradually louder:

What else can it do? Ask the children for some other ideas and then try them out.

Here are some possibilities. I have again invented my own way of writing them down:

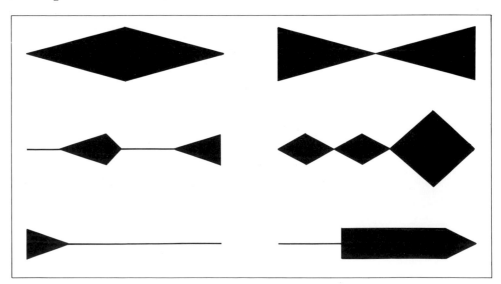

3 The voice, that most adaptable of musical instruments, can produce long and short sounds with equal ease. That is not true of all instruments. Which instruments are particularly suited to short sounds?

▶ Allow the children time to experiment with a selection of instruments. *Experimenting with sound* is what composing is all about — until we know just what instruments will and will not do, we cannot make effective use of them.

However, to turn a class of children loose to experiment with a roomful of instruments could be a recipe for disaster! Perhaps the children should divide into groups of four or five, taking two or three instruments for each group, and see what they can make of them. Then each group can show the class what it has discovered.

Individual short sounds may not be as versatile as long sounds. But all of the previous shapes can be achieved using *repeated* short notes.
E.g.

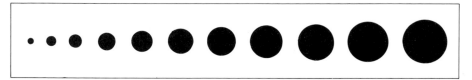

Draw some shapes on the board and ask members of the class to use their short-sound instruments to perform each of them in turn.

4 Can the class suggest a way of using long-sound and short-sound instruments to 'perform' one of the designs they invented for the curtains?

Perhaps one instrument should be chosen to represent the strokes and another to represent the dots. We could move across the paper, playing long or short sounds as we get to the strokes and dots. Or we could go round and round the paper, starting at the outside and working inwards in a spiral. We might move up and down. What do the children suggest?

Try it out with one volunteer playing long sounds and another playing short sounds.

Would it be more effective if *several* similar instruments played together each time they reached a cluster of dots? How could we treat a group of strokes?

The whole class might even perform a 'curtain' using voices and body sounds.

5 Now put away the curtains and ask someone to suggest a *musical* design.

▶ You might help the children to make the leap from visual shapes to aural shapes by suggesting a simple pattern to be performed by four children playing short sounds and one child using a long sound. Here is an example:

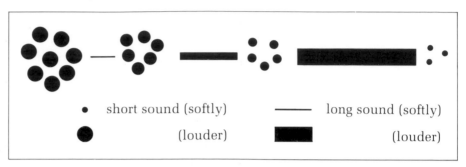

●   short sound (softly)   ——   long sound (softly)

●   (louder)   ▬▬   (louder)

When the class has grasped the idea divide the children into groups of six and give them the following rules:

— each group needs three short-sound players and three long-sound players
— the short-sound players must choose one *sort* of sound (drum sounds, wooden sounds, etc.) and the long-sound players another sort
— each group must invent a *shape* for its piece (which it can write down or not, as it wishes)
— each group must be able to play its piece twice identically.

When the children have completed their work, ask each group in turn to perform to the class.

LISTENING

At the very end of his *Young Person's Guide to the Orchestra*, Benjamin Britten makes striking use of the contrast between short notes and long notes.

After about fifteen minutes spent introducing the orchestra section by section (ending with the percussion), Britten embarks on a *tour de force* in which he builds up the entire orchestra, instrument by instrument, starting with a solitary piccolo.

Everyone is required to play as fast as possible — all notes are short. Then, at the climax of this final section of the work, the brass instruments enter playing in stately tones the tune (borrowed from Henry Purcell) that opened *Young Person's Guide*.

The simultaneous use of fast, short sounds and slow, long sounds is quite stunning!

PROJECT 3 Rough sounds and smooth sounds

> **66** *A huge bear crashes through the forest. Its movements are relentlessly powerful; no creature dares to stand in its way. Yet even this great bear stops in fear as venomous snakes slither across its path.*
>
> *The snakes disappear into the undergrowth and the bear crashes on.* **99**

LISTENING

Before starting the creative part of this project, listen to the very beginning of 'Mars', the first of *The Planets* by Gustav Holst. Like the bear in the scenario, Holst's music is relentlessly powerful.

1 Can the children identify what it is that gives the music its powerful drive?

> ▶ I feel that it is achieved by seemingly endless repetition of the eight-note rhythm played by the strings and timpani. Additional weight comes from the heavy sustained notes of the horns and woodwind.

2 Listen to the first thirty seconds of Holst's music once more. Then, without further discussion, divide the class into groups of six and ask each group to invent a *repeating rhythm* that will capture the relentless power of the bear's movements. The children may only use their voices or body sounds, e.g., clapping hands, slapping chests, etc.

Unlike Holst's music, the children's music must be *rough* as well as powerful. Perhaps they could invent a body movement to go with the rhythm and so add to the sense of roughness and power.

3 Ask each group to perform to the class and discuss the merits of each performance. Would the children like to return to their groups and make some minor adjustments in the light of this discussion?

The snakes, by contrast, slither sinuously out of the undergrowth.

LISTENING

Return to 'Mars'. In the middle of the piece, after about 2′45″, comes some frantic scampering by wind and strings and then a great chord. Then the music starts again, sinuously and quietly.

4 Listen to this quiet music with the children. What makes the music sinuous?

▶ Holst creates this effect by:
 – making the bassoon/cello/double bass melody crawl around adjacent notes — the melody hardly ever leaps
 – never altering the rhythm.
 He further adds to the atmosphere of suspense by making the violins tremble continuously on a single note.

5 When the children have listened to Holst's sinuous music, ask them to invent some of their own.

First they must choose a suitable instrument. As so often, the voice may prove the most suitable — it can slide around in the most 'snaky' way. Which instruments can achieve the effect of sliding from note to note?

▶ Violins, cellos, and trombones are the orchestral instruments that can slide most effectively. A keyboard with a bend-wheel or a swanee whistle can do the same. But Holst didn't ask his players to *slide*, simply to move smoothly from note to note. Recorders and other wind instruments can do this.

6 Choose a suitable instrument and ask a volunteer to invent a smooth, sinuous melody. Remember the rules:
 – the melody can only move to adjacent notes
 – the rhythm must never alter.

▶ Here is a sinuous melody to be played on a metallophone. Follow the numbers. The notes are quite slow and are all of equal length. The beater should be soft:

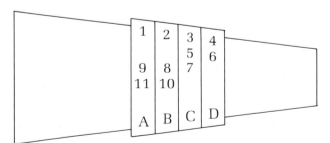

How would it sound if somebody accompanied the sinuous melody by trembling continuously on one note (as Holst's violins did)? This might be done using two beaters on one note of a xylophone; or the children might think another instrument more suitable.

7 Ask the children to return to their groups and nominate one member of the group to invent a smooth snake-melody. Perhaps they could invent two snake-melodies and play them simultaneously so that they intertwine as snakes do in real life.

   ▶ Visit each group to see how work is progressing and, when appropriate, move them on to assembling the complete piece:

Bear music   Snake music   Bear music

8 Ask each group to perform its completed piece. If the children need to change instruments between bear and snake music, this must be done quietly and efficiently so as not to spoil the effect of the music. Professional percussion players lay discarded instruments and beaters on a soft cloth so that the changeover makes no sound at all.

LISTENING

When the children have completed the project, play the complete 'Mars' to them. It will help their concentration if you first explain the structure of Holst's music. It is precisely the same shape as the children have used, though on a grander scale:

ROUGH MUSIC	wind and strings scampering, BIG CHORD	SMOOTH MUSIC	ROUGH MUSIC	wind and strings scampering, BIG CHORDS

PROJECT 4 High sounds and deep sounds

This project is about contrasting character in melodies. It could even be described as a duet between an elephant and a mouse!

The activity is designed for children working in pairs.

▶ I use the word 'deep' in the title, rather than the word 'low', because there is constant and universal confusion in primary school children's minds about the meaning of *low* in a musical context. Perhaps because of the ubiquitous use of the phrases 'turn it down' and 'low volume' the word is frequently taken to mean 'soft'. In musical parlance it always means 'deep'.

 This project might develop out of work in science, looking at the way creatures move.

1 Ask the children which moves faster, an elephant or a mouse. In my experience children will reply that a mouse does. Yet I would give odds on the elephant winning a race across open ground!

The mouse may, however, move faster *relative to its size*. A mouse scuttling across the floor might even give an impression of greater speed than a cheetah (the fastest creature on earth) racing across the open plains.

In general, smaller animals' hearts beat faster than those of larger animals, and in consequence their lives are shorter. However, it would take a great deal of excitement to increase the sluggish pace of the heart of a tortoise!

Do tortoises live a short time or a long time?

How many other exceptions can the children find to the generalization that smaller creatures move relatively faster than larger creatures and live shorter lives?

▶ I have started the project in this rather curious way because I have found a parallel expectation in music, i.e., that tunes played on small instruments with high notes will move quickly, while those played on large, deep instruments will move slowly. You only have to listen to a solo euphonium player in a good brass band to know that this is another unsafe generalization!

2 Ask the children to imagine that they are watching a nature film about a mouse. Their job is to invent the music for the film.
– what sort of melody would be suitable?
– should it be slow and thoughtful or quick and neat?
– should it be played on a high-pitched instrument or a deep one?

▶ The children are certain to opt for a high-pitched instrument. Take a glockenspiel and remove all the bars except G, A, C, D, and E.

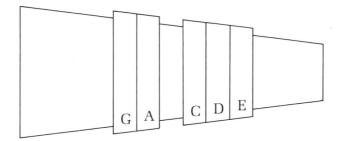

Ask a volunteer to come and invent a tiny fragment of mouse-melody. It must last no longer than six notes (the mouse is very small), and the child must be able to remember it and play it again identically.

▶ I praise whatever the child invents — confidence is all-important — and immediately ask the child to repeat the phrase. If this proves difficult, I say, 'Now invent something so simple that you can remember it and play it again easily.'

Repetition, of course, makes the melody twice as long; a much easier way of extending material than inventing something new.

3 When two or three children have invented fragments of mouse-melody in front of the class, return to the idea of the film.
The scene changes to an elephant lumbering through the jungle.

▶ Set up a deep-sounding instrument — a bass xylophone is ideal (or an ordinary one will do) — with all the bars removed except G, A, B, D, and E.

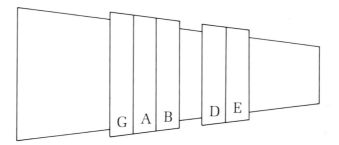

How should the character of the elephant's music differ from that of the mouse? Should it be:
– faster or slower
– neater or more ponderous
– louder or softer?

▶ A ponderous character can be achieved in a number of ways, including playing slowly, constantly returning to the same note, repeating notes.

Ask for a volunteer to invent a short elephant melody applying the same rules about simplicity as before.

4 Now ask everyone to choose a partner. Each pair must invent a short musical conversation between an elephant and a mouse which can be remembered and performed twice.

> ▶ CAUTION. There is a risk that some of the children will find it difficult to know when to stop and will invent a long string of meandering phrases.
>
> Help the class by first making clear the sort of musical shape you expect each conversation to take. You might, for example, use two of the volunteers who have already invented melodies to put together a short symmetrical conversation:

| **Mouse:** | fragment 1 | | fragment 1 | |
| **Elephant:** | | fragment A | | fragment A |

| **Mouse:** | fragment 2 | | fragment 1 |
| **Elephant:** | | fragment A | |

> Despite the mouse's best endeavour to extend the conversation, the elephant refuses to say anything more!
>
> ▶ It is unlikely that you will have enough instruments or enough space for all of the pairs to work on this project at the same time. One practical way of running the project is to release pairs of children from lessons throughout the day to go off and invent their conversations. Place a time limit on the exercise and make it clear that each pair will perform to the class when they return.

5 If the project proves productive you might like to take it one stage further. Instead of one child remaining silent while the other plays, ask each child to invent an accompaniment to the other's melody. This must be *extremely* simple so as not to detract from the importance of the melody. It might involve:
- using one repeated note as an accompaniment
- picking up another instrument (perhaps a drum or a triangle) to use as an accompanying instrument
- clapping or humming as the melody is played.

LISTENING

When the children have completed their pieces return to Britten's *Young Person's Guide to the Orchestra* and play the double bass variation to them. This is immediately before the harp variation.

Britten's music is not a conversation (the double basses are always the soloists), but it does exploit the contrast between high sounds and deep sounds. The high sounds (flutes, oboes, bassoons) are always the accompanists.

To show just how carefully Britten constructs his variation, here is a graphic score of the music:

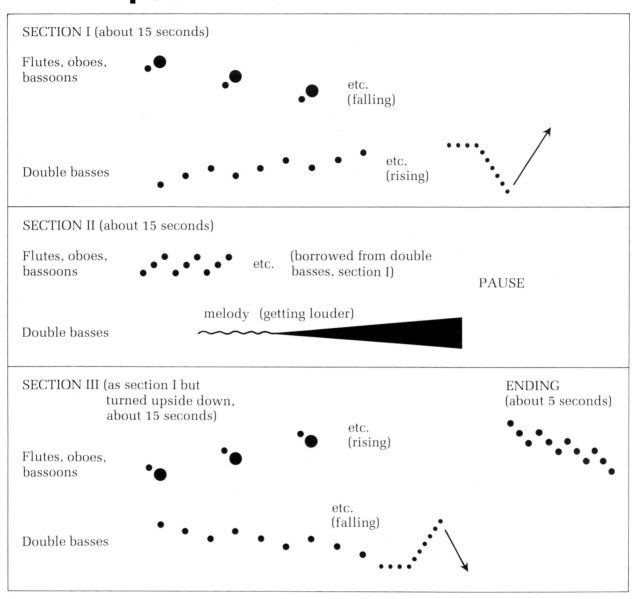

For additional high 'mouse' music try:
    'Chinese Dance' from *The Nutcracker Suite* (Casse Noisette) by Tchaikovsky.

For elephant music try:
    'The Elephant' from *Carnival of the Animals* by Saint-Saëns.

CHAPTER FOUR

Ceremonies

THIS CHAPTER IS ABOUT:

Important and less-important sounds
Simple melody
Movement, slowness, stillness, gesture, appearance
Control, co-ordination, economy.

▶ The chapter begins with two projects that are designed to introduce the children to the concepts of ceremonial movement and ceremonial music.

You could launch these projects with your own *ceremony*. Wait in the hall or classroom, suspended cymbal and beater ready, while a colleague stands with your class outside. Then, with massive dignity, open the doors, strike the cymbal twice, and with ceremonial gestures (and in absolute silence) lead half of the class to one place in the hall and seat them. With another two cymbal strokes turn to the remaining children. . . .

Think about ceremonies.

Chinese New Year

56

In a ceremony we must think about how we *move*. We may have to move in a slow, controlled way — or we may need to stand totally still and quiet.

Probably we will have to think about our appearance. We may have to dress up in an unusual way.

Ceremonies are frequently made up of blocks of movement, blocks of music, blocks of spectacle. Groups of people may need to act in a very controlled, co-ordinated way.

May Day in Red Square

Individuals may also need to act in quite a different way from normal.

PROJECT 1 Ceremonial pairs

1 Ask a volunteer to perform an everyday task — giving books out to the class, opening the door for a friend — in a ceremonial fashion.

How did it differ from the usual way?

Discuss with the class the differences between everyday behaviour and ceremonial behaviour.

▶ If you performed the ceremony suggested at the beginning of the chapter, you will have another example to discuss. Ask the child to re-enact the giving out of books or the opening of the door, and help him or her to slow the movements down and formalize the procedure into a series of stylized actions, explaining to the class as you go along.

2 Ask each child to choose a partner and to work out a brief scene in which both partners behave *ceremonially*. And give them one rule — only one of them may move at any one time.

Let each pair show its ceremonial scene to the class.

Discuss the scenes with the class. Did the children notice that each ceremonial exchange consisted of *important key gestures* (the actual giving of the book, the opening of the door) and *less-important* ones (e.g., walking from one place to another)? Can the children remember some of the *important* gestures that their friends made when they performed?

3 We can invent music to accompany these ceremonial actions.

Could the class choose an *important sound?* And could a volunteer, or volunteers, practise playing it?

> ▶ CAUTION: Be careful not to impose *your* ideas here, unless your pupils are completely stuck. *You* may feel that a gong (if you have one!), a clash of cymbals or a heavy chord on the piano are 'important' sounds. But what do the children suggest?

Now ask the class to choose a *less-important sound.*

> ▶ You may immediately think of the jingle of sleigh-bells or the 'ting' of a triangle, but the above caution applies here too!

4 Choose a pair of children to perform their scene again. Could someone accompany their *important movements* with the *important sound* and their *less-important movements* with the *less-important sound?*

> ▶ It may be that the *less-important sound* has to be played to accompany extended movements like walking. Have the children chosen a sound that can be extended, e.g., by continuously shaking sleigh bells or ringing a triangle?

There is always the possibility of using silence.

5 Now ask each pair to decide on an *important sound* and a *less-important sound* and to develop the ceremonial scene they have already invented by adding the two sorts of sound. The children must be both actors *and* musicians, making their music as they perform their ceremonies.

When the pairs of children have all performed their mini-ceremonies to the class, they might discuss ways of combining to make grander and longer ceremonies.

PROJECT 2 Building-music

1 Look at some pictures of buildings designed for ceremonial use.

Greek Temple

Mosque

Cathedral

You might be able to visit a local church, temple or even the Law Courts or Town Hall.

How does the design of these buildings differ from the design of our homes? What would they be like to live in? What do you think were the architects' aims in designing them in this way?

Buildings

Most ceremonial buildings are public rather than private, probably with wide-open spaces instead of individual private rooms. On the whole they are built on a grander scale, designed to impress, perhaps even to intimidate. They look serious and important.

---

2 Show the class the way in which architects draw their plans from different perspectives.

The above picture of the Greek temple shows a front elevation. Could the children draw a plan of the temple as they imagine it from above, showing the layout of the floor area? The pillars are not simply there to support the roof. What other function might they have?

▶ Here is the floor plan as I imagine it. When you enter the building, the pillars draw your eyes to the altar.

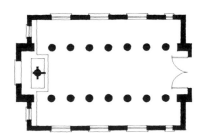

3 Ask the children to design their own public building and draw a front elevation and floor plan. Perhaps they would like to work in pairs, so that each child has the opportunity of discussing ideas with a friend.

4 Think about the sort of music we might invent to accompany a procession entering the Greek temple or a building that the children themselves have designed.

In the previous project we explored *important* and *less-important sounds*. We could use *important sounds* again in a structural way rather like the pillars of the Greek temple. Could we find a use for some *less-important sounds*, possibly as links between successive *important sounds*?

If people are to process in a dignified way whilst our music is played, it may be appropriate for the music to have a stately pulse or rhythm.

Could we also find an effective use for silence in our music?

> ▶ By keeping the idea of procession and dignity to the fore, a certain character of sound-invention may well emerge. And the image of the pillars in the Greek temple may be helpful, perhaps suggesting a slow, dignified rhythm. But even more important is the concept of *important sounds* linked by *less-important sounds* that we explored in Project 1. This can be a key way of giving a sequence of sounds some shape and making it satisfying.

5 Divide the children into groups of six and visit each group as it works on its processional music.

> ▶ If you find a group that has decided which sounds to use but is at a loss to know how to proceed, you might perhaps suggest a simple alternation of *important* and *less-important sounds*. Try not to inject new ideas; rather, help the children to find a way of using what they already have. Remember that ceremonial music is often extraordinarily simple, relying for its effect on the support of spectacle.

6 When each group has performed its music to the class, the groups could work in pairs, one group devising a ceremony to perform to the other group's music, and vice versa.

Gods of the Ancient World

The two previous projects concentrated on the simple dignity of ceremonial music and movement. The next two projects in this chapter take a legend as a starting-point. I have chosen legends that have proved particularly fruitful with primary school children, using music and spectacle on an equal footing.

PROJECT 3 Shamash

Shamash (centre) rising between two mountains

Shamash

Shamash was the Babylonian sun-god of justice. According to legend, scorpion-people appeared every morning to open the great doors in the Mountain in the East. Shamash appeared through the doors and climbed the mountain to his waiting coach. Throughout the day he was driven across the sky, and in the evening arrived at the Mountain in the West, disappearing at nightfall through doors in the mountain.

During the hours of darkness Shamash travelled underground, back to the Mountain in the East, ready to emerge again the next day.

1 Discuss the legend with the class.
Why does Shamash emerge from the Mountain in the East in the morning and disappear into the Mountain in the West at nightfall? And why did the Babylonians imagine that the god travelled underground during the night?

2 Suggest to the class the idea of turning the legend into a ceremony. Can they imagine the ancient Babylonians commemorating this story in honour of Shamash?

Before inventing details of movement or music, can the children suggest a shape or layout for the ceremony?

▶ This ceremony could involve a circular ritual in the school hall. The class could process round the hall from the Mountain in the East to the Mountain in the West and complete the circle to return to their starting-point.

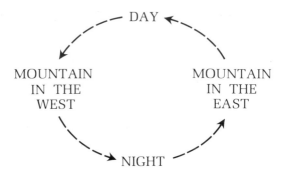

But rather than immediately suggesting this idea to the children, ask them for their own ideas.

3 Then we must decide on a *musical* shape for the ceremony. Where should we place the *important sounds*? They will be important in establishing its musical shape.

▶ For instance, an *important sound* might be used to herald the opening of the doors in the mountains.

4 Most of our music will be used to *accompany the procession* from one mountain to the other. This music will be less important than the door-opening sounds.

Ask a volunteer to choose any note on a xylophone and to play a steady pulse — as steady as the ticking of a clock. Ask the child to play at the speed our feet would move if we were walking in a dignified procession.

Ask another volunteer to come and add another note, playing exactly in time with the first child.

The second child may wish to try out one or two different notes before deciding on the one that he or she likes.

▶ There are no rules about what sounds satisfactory. It is purely a matter for the child to decide.

Encourage the children to watch each other as they play. This will help them to play exactly together.

Invite a third child to add another note in the same way, then a fourth. Then ask the class to suggest a neat way of finishing the march.

> ▶ The players could simply stop. Or they might drop out, one at a time. They might fade away; there are many possibilities. They could try out several ideas and the class could vote on the most effective.

5 Divide the class into groups of four and ask each group to invent its own *processional march*, with each child using one note only.

> ▶ Some groups may decide to use xylophones (four children can easily sit around one instrument); others might use untuned instruments like claves, Indian bells, etc.

This will be the simple, dignified music that accompanies the ceremonial pulling of Shamash's coach from the Mountain in the East to the Mountain in the West. In ceremonial music it is often the simplest music that makes the greatest impression.

6 When each group has performed to the class, ask the children to think about ways of making one march from all of their music.

> ▶ If all the groups decide to play simultaneously, the music may sound more powerful, like a stadium full of people doing a slow handclap.
>
> If the groups alternate, the music may be less powerful but more varied.

There are also some practical matters to be considered.

Some members of the class will have to be free to enact the pulling of the coach. Perhaps only two or three groups should play their music, leaving the other children free to move.

7 We may need ceremonial music for Shamash's *night journey* back to the East. It might be effective to play 'brighter' sounding music for the day time procession, and 'darker' music for the night-time procession.

> ▶ 'Darkness' in music is discussed in Miniatures, Project 1. It is often felt to be synonymous with deeper sounds (see the Listening section at the end of this project). 'Lightness' may be evoked by higher sounds. Thus a children's march played on bass xylophone might be considered 'darker' than one played on a glockenspiel.

Have the children already by chance created some pieces that sound darker than others? Or would they like to make appropriate adjustments? Perform a 'dark' march followed by a 'light' march.

8 The children must now decide on the sort of *movements* the coach-pullers will make. If they are simply going to march in a row, the steady pulse of the one-note march will do admirably. But if more exotic movements are envisaged, a less symmetrical pulse might be more suitable.

As an example, sing the first line of 'London Bridge is falling down' to the class. Then clap the jagged rhythm of the first two notes:

Lon-don   Lon-don   Lon-don   Lon-don
—   •   —   •   —   •   —   •

How might somebody move to this sort of rhythm?

Should the *night* coach-pullers *move* in a different way to the *day* coach-pullers and, therefore, have a different rhythm for their music?

9 Perform the day music with movement, then change over, musicians becoming actors and actors becoming musicians, for the night procession.

When we assemble the complete ceremony this changeover will need careful stage-management. The musicians cannot simply drop instruments and scramble into their acting positions. Perhaps the gradual entry of one player after another in the original march holds the key to an appropriate ceremonial changeover. Can the children devise a way of doing it?

Now the ceremony is almost complete. Individuals will be needed to play the *important sounds* and the class will have to decide where these performers should stand with their instruments.

10 One last musical decision.

Endings are important. They are the 'final touch' and they are the last impression that the audience takes away with them. How should the ceremony finish?

11 Try out the complete ceremony with music.

Now the class might like to turn its attention to *costume*.

▶ Costume and particularly masks help us all to enter more easily into an imaginary world. They help to dispel inhibition—people will do things in a mask that they would not entertain in other circumstances, hence the masked-balls of old Venice and many other places!

12 You may decide to perform the completed ceremony to the school. The audience could sit at one end of the hall or it might sit in the spaces not being used by the performers, so that the ceremony takes place all around it. Perhaps the children could devise a simple ceremony to lead the audience to their places.

LISTENING

Ceremony is the very essence of the music of the French composer Olivier Messiaen (born 1908). Almost all of his music is conceived in blocks, one self-contained section of music followed by another, punctuated usually by silence. Rarely does one musical idea grow out of another, as it does with virtually every other Western composer.

For example:

DRAMATIC MUSIC	QUIET MELODY	GONGS
QUIET MELODY	DRAMATIC MUSIC	

Listen to the first movement of *Et Expecto Resurrectionem Mortuorum* for wind, brass, and percussion instruments. Like all of Messiaen's music this piece is an expression of the composer's deep Christian faith.

As complementary listening to the children's *dark* music the opening of *Et Expecto* could scarcely be bettered. The darkest instruments of the orchestra, three bassoons, contra bassoon, bass trombone, tuba, contrabass tuba, and gongs parade in stately dignity. They are later joined by woodwind and horns.

At the end of the movement come eight of the most *important sounds* the children will ever hear. Brass and gongs blaze, echoed always a fraction later by woodwind and higher percussion.

Listen also to the beginning of the second movement. A brief attention-grabbing flurry of wind is immediately followed by the stillness of quiet chords played by horns and clarinets.

Then a wonderful example of changing colour in music: a single melody weaves its calm, processional way through a series of different instruments — first oboe, then clarinet, then the combined colours of oboe, cor anglais, clarinet, and bassoon.

A block of active music follows. Then the melodic procession continues.

Messiaen's music is, in fact, a ceremony without movement.

PROJECT 4 The August Personage of Jade

The August Personage of Jade

Each year in ancient China, a great ceremony took place in the Temple of Heaven in Beijing. The Emperor was carried in a ceremonial chair accompanied by dignitaries, soldiers, dancers, and musicians to offer silk, jade, and the finest foods to a ceremonial fire lit in honour of the August Personage of Jade, the Father of Heaven.

The August Personage had created mankind by modelling human beings out of clay. As he finished each model, it was put in the sun to dry. Some were damaged by rain while they were still soft. They became the ill and handicapped in the world.

The August Personage was always represented as an old man in a ceremonial costume decorated with embroidered dragons. But he was said to be able to transform himself into seventy two different shapes!

He lived with his family in a palace guarded by Wang, whose badge of office was a great stick.

This Chinese legend offers a wealth of material for ceremonies projects. Here is a framework. Help the children to fill in the details.

This project might be linked to some work on different religions.

1 How does this Chinese version of creation compare with that of other religions? And how does it compare with modern scientific theories of evolution?

The idea of making clay models of people might lead into some work on the fascinating Tomb Warriors found in Xi'an. What do the children imagine was the thinking behind the making of thousands of life-sized model soldiers and then burying them in rows around a tomb?

Tomb Warriors, Xi'an, China

2 Enact a scene in which the children are clay figures which gradually come alive.

Introduce the idea by demonstrating total *stillness* to the class. You must stand as still as a statue. If anyone sees any part of you move they are to put up their hands.

Ask a child to say 'Go' and then you freeze. After a few seconds give the tiniest twitch of an eye or a finger. Every hand should shoot up!

▶ Curiously, as every actor and dancer knows, the stiller a person or a group of people is, the more every tiny movement shows.

3 Divide the class in half and ask the two halves to sit on the floor facing one another. On an agreed signal, one half will freeze whilst the other half watches for any movement. Then let the motionless group become the watchers.

Now ask the class to create a tableau of clay figures starting with total stillness and silence. Some of the clay figures might be standing, some sitting, some lying down. Can the figures *gradually* come to life? How slowly can this be achieved?

4 Could the coming-to-life be accompanied by sounds made only with our bodies? We might click fingers as each tiny movement is made, starting imperceptibly and intensifying as our movements increase.

Try out the finger-clicking idea with the children. Would they prefer to use an alternative sound or sounds?

5 Can someone now suggest an *important sound* that could be made when the coming-to-life sounds are at their most intense? It might come from Wang, who guards the palace of the August Personage with his great stick of office. It could signal that the coming-to-life is completed.

A moment of absolute silence might follow.

6 Then a procession begins.

The legend tells us that the Emperor was carried on a ceremonial chair accompanied by dignitaries, soldiers, dancers, and musicians. We could invent one piece of music that combines elements of dignified, military, and dance music. And everyone could play it.

First a Chinese melody.

▶ Chinese music is based on a scale of five notes — the pentatonic scale. If you play on the black notes of the piano without ever straying onto the white notes, you are using a pentatonic scale.

Set up this pentatonic scale on a xylophone:

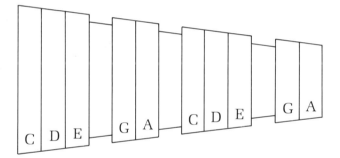

Could someone invent a short tune that would be suitable for marching using only the five *lower* notes in the diagram? Perhaps someone should march across the room like a soldier, stamping feet to demonstrate the pulse of a march.

▶ If the child has difficulty starting, you might suggest a simple progression note by note, from C up to A and back again, playing one note to each pulse of the marching feet. Then the child might be encouraged to move more quickly across one or two of the notes, and so vary the rhythm a little.

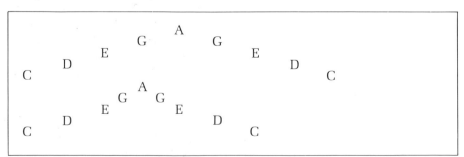

7 Once the child has invented a simple fragment of march tune (eight notes will do), ask him or her to repeat it to make the music twice as long.

> ▶ Don't hesitate to encourage the children to extend their music by repetition. It is the most common of all the devices used by composers to extend their musical material.

Ask another child to invent a new section of march using the five *top* notes in the diagram, and again to lengthen it by repeating.

8 Can anyone suggest a way of using these two fragments of melody to make one complete march tune?

> ▶ A B A shape (child 1, child 2, child 1), a sort of musical sandwich, is one of the most common musical shapes ever devised by man (see the Listening section at the end of this project). Its symmetry has the same satisfying feeling of order and security as two pillars and a pediment in architecture.

9 When the two march composers have arrived at a version of their tune that satisfies them, send them away to teach a group of friends to play the tune, *Chinese style*. The friends may play any melodic instruments they choose.

> ▶ When we in the West accompany a tune, we think in terms of chords (e.g., a song with guitar chords). Chinese musicians do not think in this way. When they add musicians to a piece, the new players also play the tune; nobody plays chords. Chinese music gets its richness from the ornamental notes that each player adds to the tune during the performance. Any true accompaniment is played on untuned percussion instruments.

When the march players perform their music, it too may be enriched by the odd different note, perhaps played by mistake. But this will not matter; when we use the pentatonic scale, all the notes seem to fit well with each other.

10 Meanwhile discuss *dignity* with the class.

How do dignified people move? The children might try devising a dignified procession, paying special attention to the way they move.

Could someone choose a *dignified sound* and play it slowly and repeatedly as the procession moves?

▶ The children may well feel that deep sounds are more dignified than high sounds, e.g., a slow pulse on a large drum, bass xylophone or cello.

11 When the march group returns, ask the dignified-sound player(s) to find a way of fitting their music with the march. Perhaps the dignified sound(s) should only be heard every four pulses of the march; or the children might think of some other way.

12 Ask for a group of volunteers to take the part of soldiers in the ceremony. Could they choose portable instruments that could be played as they march? Perhaps they should practise sitting down and playing with the march tune before they try to march and play simultaneously!

▶ Small drums and cymbals are suitably portable and martial. Or should Chinese soldiers play something more exotic?

Don't let the soldiers play too loudly.

Perform the march with its added dignified and military sounds. Could the dignitaries *and* the soldiers process, each going at an appropriate pace?

13 The last group of participants in the Chinese ceremony were dancers.

Ask some of the children to invent their own Chinese dance. It might incorporate such 'oriental' gestures as bowing with hands together. Or you may be lucky enough to have a child in your class who knows how Chinese dancers *really* dance. If not, you may be sure that the children will have their own ideas of how it should look!

Eastern dancers sometimes carry small instruments whose sounds become an integral part of the dance. Indian dancers, for example, strap bunches of tiny bells to their wrists and ankles so that any movement they make generates its own music. Could the children choose light instruments to hold as they dance?

14 The class has now assembled the ingredients of the ceremony. Can the children suggest how it might best be organized?

Here is one possible format. Imagine you are looking down on the ceremony from the ceiling of the hall.

1. Children (✘) spread around the hall as clay people drying.
One child as the August Personage, one as Wang.

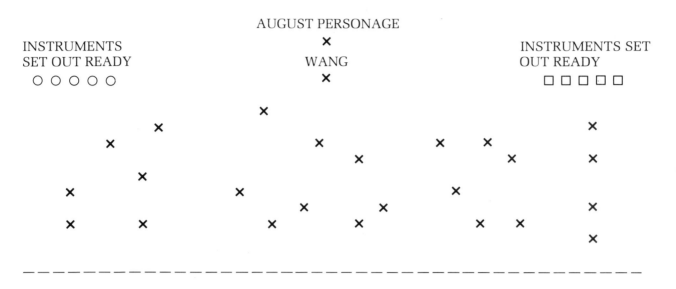

2. Important sound. Children begin to come alive and move into their positions as musicians, dancers, dignitaries, and soldiers.

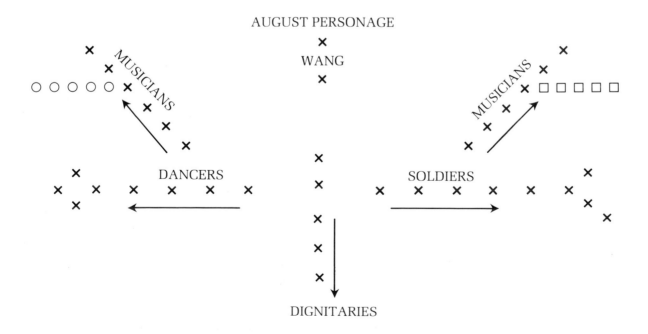

3. Important sound. Musicians begin to play and a child representing the Emperor is carried in by the dignitaries.

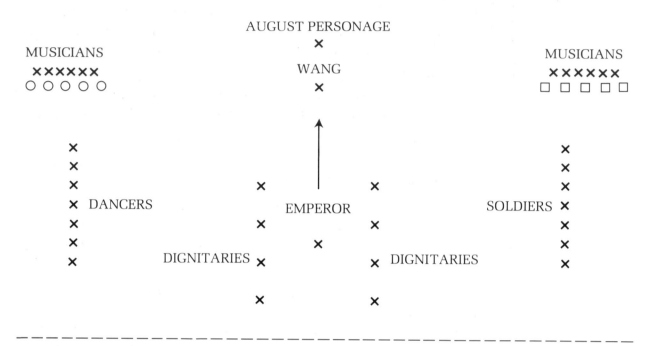

4. Important sound. Musicians play. Soldiers approach the August Personage adding their music as they move (A). Important sound. Musicians play. Dancers approach the August Personage adding their music as they move (B).

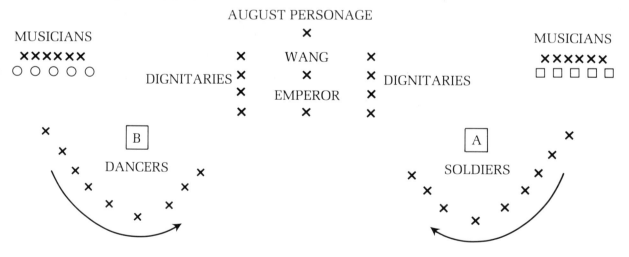

To finish, everyone plays simultaneously.

LISTENING

First of all, you should perhaps try to listen to some genuine Chinese music. Recordings are readily available in many of our big cities and from good libraries. What you want is *traditional* music, which may be played by a traditional Chinese orchestra. Beware of Chinese pop music which is more or less the same as ours!

Chinese music has appealed to many Western composers. In 1908 the French composer Maurice Ravel completed the music for a ballet called *Ma Mère l'Oye* (Mother Goose). It was first performed in Paris in 1915.

Nowadays it is usual to hear five short pieces which Ravel extracted from the ballet music and called *Ma Mère l'Oye: Cinq Pièces Enfantines.* They are known as the *Mother Goose* Suite.

The third of these pieces, 'Laideronnette, Empress of the Pagodas' is a pastiche of Chinese music and makes excellent supplementary listening to this project. It uses the pentatonic scale throughout, and is constructed in the A B A form discussed on page 69.

The two A sections are built out of a swift tune first heard on the piccolo. The B section (after about 1 minute) is both dignified and wistful. The dignified music is characterized by the periodic use of a gong and a wonderful combination of musical colours—low clarinet, harp, and celeste (a metallophone with piano keyboard). The wistful music is played by the flute.

The return to the A music is managed with consummate skill. Whilst the dignified B music is still playing, the celeste slides in with the swift A tune on top of it. Then the piccolo and flute take up the swift tune and the dignified music fades away. The flow of the music is never interrupted. But then Ravel was an extraordinarily good composer!

I would thoroughly recommend all five movements of *Mother Goose* Suite for classroom listening.

CHAPTER FIVE

The seasons

THIS CHAPTER IS ABOUT:

Collage

Washes of background texture

Evocative foreground fragments *of sound*

Putting sounds together

Musical structure

Collage

The French word 'collage' (literally 'a pasting') was coined by artists early in this century to describe a new sort of visual art—the gluing of found objects (pieces of wood, metal, scraps of photographs, fabric, etc.) to a background to create an abstract picture. The word is now part of the English language and may equally be applied to music as to the visual arts.

▶ I have found the four seasons of the year extremely fruitful subjects for musical collage. And I like to relate the children's completed work to *The Four Seasons* by Vivaldi. I have indicated ways of doing this at appropriate points in this chapter.

PROJECT 1 Autumn

▶ This project might be started in the autumn term without any prior reference to collage.

1 Think about autumn.

At this time of year the northern hemisphere tilts away from the sun. This has a profound effect on living things — the slowing of the sap in plants, the slowing of the metabolism in creatures.

How has this slowing-down of life affected the forest in the picture? Could the children describe some of the things that have happened to the autumn forest?

Perhaps one of the children could describe a walk in the forest in autumn. Or you may even be able to take the class into a wood or forest. How might it differ from a summer walk? The dry leaves might *crackle* underfoot, while those still attached to the trees might *rustle* in the wind.

▶ Here you could digress into a discussion about onomatopoeia. Ask the children to think of any words that are descriptive in their sound. You might then narrow the field to words that could be used in a description of autumn, making a list of the children's words on the board.

2 Ask the children to write short poems about autumn, inviting them to include a few (but not too many!) onomatopoeic words in their verse.

Share the poems with the class.

3 Divide the class into groups of six and ask each group to choose one of its members' poems to read in chorus. Explain that the poem is to be performed quietly, except for the onomatopoeic words which should be exploited for their sound. Perhaps the children should take it in turns to say the onomatopoeic words:

all children: The dry leaves   in the   wind
solo child 1:   whirled
solo child 2:   chilling

or perhaps they can think of another way of making these words special.

Ask each group to perform to the class.

The poem is now half-way to being a piece of *word-music*. It is no longer so important that we hear every word, it is the expressiveness of the special words that makes the performance effective.

4 Discuss the idea of *collage* with the class. Point out that what the children have just performed is a sort of verbal collage — a few key words 'glued' prominently onto the background of the rest of the poem.

> Here you might like to put the poems aside for a while and digress into visual collage. The children could make their own collection of autumn things in readiness to create a collage to hang on the wall.
>
> Help the class to make a *background texture* onto which to glue their collage items. A piece of card lightly glued and then dusted with fine sand would make a good background texture for a summer collage. What do the children think would be an appropriate background for an autumn collage?

5 When the class has finished its art work and made an autumn collage, return for a last time to the children's autumn poems. Now the task is for each group of six to use material from *all six* of its poems to make an autumn word-collage.

Remind the children of the *background texture* they made for the art-collage. How might the words of their poems be used to create a suitable *background texture* for the word-collage? What if:
- each member of the group simply read his or her poem quietly in succession?
- all the poems were quietly read simultaneously?
- individuals read short phrases from their poems leaving gaps for others to fill in with their own phrases?
- what other possibilities are there?

How should the onomatopoeic words be 'glued' onto this background? Should:
- somebody be chosen as a *soloist* to say all the foreground words?
- each person 'perform' their own onomatopoeic words as they get to them?
- a special order of words and people be decided upon for the 'solo' words?
- some other effective way be found?

6 Divide the children into their groups to rehearse.

▶ I would wander between groups and encourage the children to get the *background texture* really soft. You may find that initially the onomatopoeic words come thick and fast! Help the children to thin them out so that they really make an impact. They may also need some help with their diction to turn the special words into expressive sounds. But beware of injecting too many of your ideas into what they are doing.

7   Ask each group to perform its finished collage to the class.

Could the whole class find a way of assembling one huge collage from elements of each group's work?

> ▶ This is an intriguing *social* exercise. Each group may well have to sacrifice a proportion of its own collage if the composite piece is not to become over-dense or over-long. I like to remove myself from the classroom, if possible, and leave the children to it. If the class can achieve a result *without* teacher help (and teacher discipline) they have done very well indeed!
>
> They may of course feel that to combine their work simply spoils several very good pieces!

PROJECT 2 Winter

> ▶ This project aims to encourage the children to make careful choices using a *few* instrumental sounds as *foreground fragments* of sound.
>
> The *background textures* for the collage are again non-instrumental.

1   Discuss winter with the class.

> 66 *Nature has come to a standstill. Wild animals have hidden away, perhaps even hibernated. The birds no longer sing. The trees are bare. When it is really cold and icy even the water no longer moves.* 99

2   With a selection of instruments laid out in front of the class, discuss 'cold' sounds and 'warm' sounds.

> ▶ Make sure there are some metal instruments: a triangle, a pair of Indian bells, small chime bars, a glockenspiel, and some hard wooden or metal beaters amongst the collection you have chosen.

► You might begin the discussion by asking the class whether they think a low note on a xylophone, struck with a soft beater, sounds 'warm' or 'cold'. It is a safe bet that they will not find it cold! Low notes (on a recorder, a mellow keyboard sound, a middle note on the piano) are all safe warm sounds! Now throw the ball into their court. Can someone come out and find a cold sound?

3 When the children have had time to decide which sounds they think are cold, ask them to be *totally* still and silent.

66 *Imagine a still, frosty winter morning. An icicle hangs from a gutter.* 99

Ask a volunteer to choose an instrument and make one solitary sound — the sound of 'playing a note' on that icicle.
What does the class think of the choice?

4 66 *Imagine now that the sun has come out over this frosty scene. From all sides the frost glints as the sun's rays catch one tiny speck of frost and then another, and another.* 99

Can the class capture this scene in sound?

► One possible solution is to distribute metal instruments that can be made to 'ting' very quietly amongst a few members of the class, asking the players to play very occasionally and very quietly as the rest of the class sits completely silent. What ideas do the children have for creating this scene?

The cold sounds will form the *foreground fragments* of a winter collage.

5 For the *background texture*, we may only use sounds that we can make with our bodies.
How would it sound if the whole class drummed their fingers very quietly and quickly on table-tops or on the floor? Could the children imagine sitting in a bus shelter or a wooden hut listening to the rain on the roof? Could they make the rain really pour down? Now reduce it to a fine drizzle.
Ask a volunteer to come out in front of the class and control the rain.

► Hands palm-upwards might signal an increase in volume, palms downwards a decrease. What other signals can the class invent?

The conductor might like to divide the class in half and control each half with one hand.
What other ideas can the class suggest for body sounds (or vocal sounds) that would make effective *background textures*?

▶ Possibilities are myriad—whistling for wind, chattering of teeth, tapping of cheeks, clicking of fingers, etc.

6 Divide the class into groups of six and ask each group to invent a *background texture* and to choose one wintery instrumental *foreground fragment* to add to it.

7 When each group has performed to the class ask the children to find a way of assembling a collage from all of the groups' ideas.

Discuss the ways we might use the *background textures*:
- should each group perform its texture one after the other?
- should all the groups play their texture music simultaneously?
- should one texture clearly finish before the next begins or should each new texture grow out of the previous one?
- should we choose a fixed order for the textures?

▶ I like to suggest that the groups sit on the floor in a circle facing each other. In this way everybody can see everybody else and, when necessary, any group or any child can become leader of the whole class.

Now think about the *foreground fragments*:
- should each group offer its *foreground fragment* in turn?
- should these emerge at random with each child playing as and when it seems appropriate?
- should the piece remain quiet and chilly throughout?
- should the volume of sound increase as the music progresses?

▶ You will be only too aware that discussion with a large group of primary children can easily become an endless stream of new ideas! It might be a good way of working to take the first suggestion for a complete piece and *try it out*. Then discuss the advantages and drawbacks and how these might be remedied. There comes a point when all composers must stop inventing anew and decide exactly how to *use* the musical materials they have already got.

In all music the way we *end* is important. It is, after all, the last impression we leave with the listener. Ask the children to organize the ending with particular care.

LISTENING

When the project is completed you might like to play 'Winter' from *The Four Seasons* by Vivaldi to the class. If you are not already familiar with the piece, listen to it on your own first. I am confident that you need no knowledge of music whatever to follow the guidelines below.

Ask the children to listen to the first movement simply as a piece of music. Before they listen, tell them the title and nothing else. Then reveal that the piece is in fact a collage of wintery ideas. Listen again. What wintery ideas can the children find in it?

Be careful. The children may hear winter where you hear none. And they will not be wrong — we all hear music in our own unique way and what we get from it *cannot* be wrong.

Vivaldi was certain what he could hear in his music. Above the notes he wrote a detailed description of what it meant to him.

Guide the children through the music using Vivaldi's words: the opening: 'Frozen and shivering in the icy snow' — we can almost hear the players shivering!

After about thirty seconds the soloist begins to play:

'In the teeth of a cruel gale'.

Thirty seconds later everybody is heard:

'Running, stamping feet at every step'.

The second (slow) movement represents 'happy, quiet days spent by the fire whilst outside everything is soaked by rain'.

Could the plucked string accompaniment be the ceaseless dripping of water? What do the children think?

The last movement opens:

'Walking cautiously on the ice . . . taking care for fear of falling.' Then:

'Going too fast, sliding and falling down'.

What else can the children find in it?

Fascinating though this is, it is important to remember that Vivaldi was not simply writing 'Tom and Jerry' music. In the end the details are of secondary importance. What matters is that the music succeeds *as music*. So too with the children's music.

PROJECT 3 Spring

▶ In this project, the *background texture* for each group's part of the collage will represent one sort of spring weather. The children may use voices or instruments. The *foreground fragments* will be drawn from the sounds of nature.

1 Spring is a season of surprises. Discuss the different sorts of weather we might expect in spring. Glorious sunny days can be interrupted quite suddenly by April showers. Wintery frost can return and storms can blow up from nowhere.

2 In the previous project we used the idea of cold sounds as *foreground fragments*. Could we use the idea of warm sounds as a *background texture* for a spring collage?

How might we create a *warm* background?

▶ Sustained mellow sounds might prove suitable. Random overlapping notes played *very softly* on an electronic keyboard might be effective:

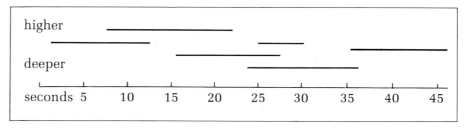

▶ Violin notes, low notes on recorders, humming, notes blown over narrow-necked bottles all sound warm. What do the children suggest?

How could the idea of a shower of rain be turned into a *background texture*? Should we use:
– many notes or few notes?
– short notes or long notes?
– high notes or deep notes?
– loud notes or soft notes?

▶ Again a random selection of notes may work best. If each child in the group takes three chime bars and plays gently and freely, the effect will almost certainly be evocative of rain. Should the players slip into a rhythm, ask them if rain *really* falls in rhythm. I suspect that they will tell you that it doesn't!

Storms are violent affairs and, you would think, scarcely suitable as *background texture*. But what about using a combination of voices and instruments to produce a *distant* storm?

▶ Using classroom instruments, a distant storm can be made to sound effective. Neither the quality of most classroom drums nor the children's playing techniques make for convincing rolls of thunder, but a distant *rumble*, using soft sticks, is quite easy to achieve. You might also try taking the bottom panel off the piano. With the right pedal depressed, try stroking your fingers across the heavy piano-wires.

Remind the children that they are only inventing *background textures*. If these become too interesting it may be difficult to hear the *foreground fragments* that will be added later.

Divide into groups to work on *background textures*.

▶ This time it may be worth considering double-sized groups, of about twelve children, as storm and rain backgrounds may need many hands and voices to be really effective. Much will depend of course on the class — large groups work much less efficiently!

3 When each group has performed its *background texture* to the class, discuss *foreground fragments*.

Everything begins to come back to life in spring. Birds, animals, and insects begin to move around again. Would they prove a fruitful source of ideas for *foreground fragments*?

Ask for volunteers to come out and try the class's suggestions as the discussion develops.

▶ The nature of birdsong is explored in detail in Miniatures, Project 4.

Think about plants. Perhaps someone would like to tackle the idea of buds swelling and bursting, and leaves unfurling.

▶ The complete collage might be best assembled by the entire class, with your help, as the *foreground* suggestions unfold.

4 Seat the class in a circle of groups (as in Miniatures Project 2) with instruments ready to perform the *background textures*. First try out some of the *foreground fragments* on top of different *background textures*. Perhaps one group should perform the sunshine texture whilst another overlays the insects. What about the birds? Which of the backgrounds will suit them best?

When the children have decided what goes best with what, help them to decide on a *shape* for their collage:
— how might we best start?
— in which order should the textures and their fragments come?
— should the general loudness (or softness) remain constant or should some part of the collage be louder than the rest?
— if the class decides to have a louder section, where should it come?

5 Perform the complete collage and discuss its effectiveness. As everyone is involved in the performance it might be difficult for the children to get a clear overall impression. Would they like to perform it to another class or teacher and see what *they* think? Or record it and then listen back to the tape.

LISTENING

Now listen to 'Spring' by Vivaldi. Again ask the children simply to listen to the music with their newly expert 'spring' ears. What can they find of spring in Vivaldi's music?

Try picking out on the recording the precise places that the children select, play the music again and see if they can explain *exactly* what the music does; for example, does Vivaldi use:
- loud or soft sounds?
- fast or slow notes?
- gentle or rough sounds?
- lots of notes or few notes?
- long notes or short notes?
- music that stays the same for a long time?
- music that contains sudden contrasts?

The opening of 'Spring' is perhaps the best known section of *The Seasons*. Immediately after the bold opening comes a long section of birdsong as 'the birds welcome spring with joyful song'.

The soloist sings first and is joined almost immediately by other solo players.

Three other sections are easily identified:
- 'Streams, breathed on by gentle winds, flow with a sweet murmur.'
- 'Now the sky is cloaked in a black mantle, and thunder and lightning herald a storm.'
- 'When all is again still the birds once more take up their sweet song.'

Each of these sections is announced by a return of the bold opening music.

Help the children to discover for themselves the *structural* use Vivaldi makes of this opening music. Listen to it once or twice to make sure that the class can recognize it easily. Then play the complete movement, asking them to raise their hands each time the opening tune recurs.

This repeated use of one musical idea as a buffer between new ideas is one of the classic ways of constructing an extended piece of music.

 # 4 Summer

▶ This project is a quodlibet—a free for all—and throws much of the musical discipline of the earlier projects to the wind!

Although this book is designed to be 'dipped into' rather than worked through laboriously, this project works best if approached *after* completing one of the previous projects in the chapter.

Begin by listening to Vivaldi's 'Summer' with the class.

LISTENING

Vivaldi's music opens 'under the merciless summer sun'—a heat so intense that the players can only bear to move slowly! The soloist is the first to move quickly, and it is at the sound of the cuckoo.

Can the children find the cuckoo in the soloist's music? (It is hidden amongst the first fast-moving notes.)

Then back to slowness and heat. Almost immediately we hear the turtledove, then the goldfinch.

The caressing music that follows this represents 'a welcome breeze'. Not welcome for long however, it swiftly develops into 'a fierce north wind'. Clearly this is an Italian, not a British summer!

The plaintive violin solo in the midst of the windy section is a shepherd-boy moaning about the weather (and fearing that he may be struck by lightning).

In the tiny second movement we meet the shepherd-boy again, trying to sleep but kept awake by 'fear of the impending thunder-storm, and by the swarms of flies and hornets'.

You might like to ask the children to suggest how Vivaldi conveys the impression of *restlessness* in his music. A peaceful melody is constantly interrupted by outbursts of vigorous music.

And in the last movement the boy's worst fears are confirmed: 'Furious thunder lights up the sky, and hail cuts down the lofty ears of corn.'

1 Think about the differences between Vivaldi's summer world and ours. Do the children think Vivaldi lived in a town or in the country?

> ▶ In fact he spent most of his life in Venice, and much of that indoors because of a health problem that had troubled him since childhood!

What things do the children like best about summer? Make a list of their ideas on the board. Which ones do they think would make good ingredients for a musical collage?

> ▶ To get a sense of the activity and excitement of summer, I would divide the children into more groups than usual (perhaps three or four in a group) so that the collage will have lots of different ingredients. You will not need a background texture.

2 Can each small group choose one activity from the list on the board and invent *six seconds* of music, sound, (or noise!) to represent it?

When each group has shown its fragment to the class and proved that it really *is* only six seconds long, discuss ways of assembling the collage.

3 Ask the children to aim for a piece that is fast and furious in which ideas come and go in a flash. *But the piece must not simply be a jumble of sound.* Perhaps someone can suggest one quiet, calm idea that can be used again and again as a *structural* device to punctuate the collage (in a way similar to the first movement of Vivaldi's 'Spring'—see Project 3).

Here is one possible structure:

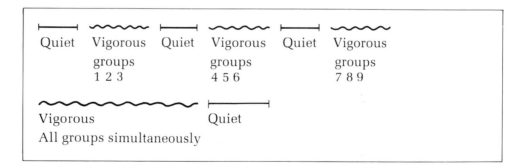

LISTENING

Here are two additional listening suggestions for *The Seasons* chapter:

'Winter' from *The Seasons* by Glazunov

Glazunov wrote this music for the ballet. It consists of six short tableaux. He obligingly stops between each one!

1 **Introduction**   Listen particularly for the swirling strings which represent the howling of the winter wind. In the middle of this tableau a beautiful flute solo is heard, accompanied at times by the chattering of teeth (short, rapidly repeated notes on string instruments).

2 **Hoar-frost**   A brittle tune is played by the wind instruments using mostly short notes. Around this the strings play smooth flowing music. I wonder if they are meant to represent the hoar-frost covering the dormant twigs of the trees? What do the children think?

3 **Ice**   This piece starts with the glistening sound of harp and celeste. Notice how the tune moves in a jerky, uneasy way as if the players were afraid of falling over.

4 **Hail**   In this tableau almost all the sounds are short. The string players are asked to tap out their notes using the wooden stick of their bows (instead of the horse-hair) to give the impression of hail drumming on a roof.

5 **Snow**   Listen to the trumpets and flutes shivering. The players create this effect by fluttering their tongues or by gargling in their throats as they blow. The tune is an elegant waltz played first by the oboe and answered by the french horn.

6 **Conclusion**   To round off his winter music in a satisfactory way, Glazunov returns to the first music we heard and rewrites it in a new, fast version.

On hearing the first cuckoo in spring by Delius

Delius captures the first warmth of spring with the sound of string instruments, helped from time to time by a few wind instruments.

How many times can the children hear the sound of the cuckoo singing? It is played by the clarinet.

CHAPTER SIX

The elements

THIS CHAPTER IS ABOUT:

Combining sounds and movements
Sensitivity, awareness, the ability to listen attentively
Inventing dramatic textures
Transforming one musical idea into another.

Elements

The ancient Greeks believed that all things were made up of four elements — earth, air, fire, and water.

Medieval scientists thought that the balance of these elements in our physical make-up determined our temperament.

We still use the word *element* for the basic chemicals or raw materials from which everything on earth is made, but we now know that there are over seventy elements, and earth, air, fire, and water are not among them!

PROJECT **1** Earth–Earth music

1 Think about earth. Not the world, not our planet, but the stuff we dig and plant things in.
    Sit in the classroom and imagine *earth*. How would we describe it? How would it feel in our hands? What would we find in it?
    Get each child to make a list of ideas about what earth is like and what it contains.

2 Next we might go out and get ourselves dirty, handling earth, digging in it, discovering what it really *does* contain.

How does what the children imagined compare with what they actually found? Make two lists side by side on the board, one headed 'We imagined' and the other headed 'We found'.

> An appropriate time to start this project, of course, is when you are doing some work on *science*. Exploration of the content of earth, perhaps even the making of a vivarium in a glass tank so that the children can watch the day-to-day activities of earthworms and the underground activities of plants, would lead naturally into the music project.

3 The task is to invent a piece of music-with-movement in three sections:

IMAGINE   REALITY   IMAGINE

In the first section, the children will become the earth and use their voices and body-sounds in a collage that tries to capture the density of earth and describes it as we *imagined* it.

In the middle section, they will become a great earth-moving machine, exploring the *reality* of earth and using the sounds of things that are found in the earth as the sound of the machine.

The piece will finish as it began, returning to the earth of our *imagination*.

▶ The first part of the project is best tackled with the whole class together. The middle section is designed for group work.

Imagine

We think of earth as dense brown stuff, a medium in which all kinds of underground activity takes place.

4 Could we create a dense, dark mass of sound using only our *voices*?

▶ Density in music is produced in exactly the same way as density in earth—a number of sounds are packed tightly together. High sounds and deep sounds are said to be far apart. So density is best achieved by using adjacent sounds.

Ask the class to sing one low-pitched note.

How would it sound if each individual sang *around* this note, going sometimes a little above it and sometimes a little below?

The effect might be a very dense sound, like the inside of a beehive.

5 Try singing to 'lah', then try humming. Does the *way* we sing affect the density of the sound? Perhaps a volunteer should listen to our experiments without joining in and decide what is most effective.

Can we find any *body sounds* that are dense? If everybody clicked fingers, for example, the sound would be dense, but would it be evocative of earth? Could we find a deeper sound?

6 Now ask the class to make *themselves* dense. Clear the centre of the classroom or school hall so that the children can get together in a tight huddle. Would it be better to stand up or to hunch together on the floor?

Ask the children to get into their 'dense position' and very quietly to start making their dense sounds. Do they think they should start with the vocal or the body sound? Should both sounds happen together or separately? If there is a silence between them, the sense of density may be lost.

7 When the sound is really dense and really soft we could introduce a new sound. Suggest that someone says one of the words or phrases from the 'We imagined' list so that it can clearly be heard over the dense *background* sound.

Then another child might say another word, then another.

These are the first *foreground* events stuck onto our collage. If the class has decided to huddle, each speaker could sit suddenly upright, say the collage word, and then return to the huddle. If the class has decided to stand, some other way will have to be found. What do the children think?

Reality

Someone watching the earth collage would get a strong impression of *mystery*. The next section is one of stark reality.

8 Ask the children to imagine that they are *robots*. Working in pairs they must invent a task that could be undertaken by two robots working out their own robotic movements.

Let each pair perform to the class. Could one or two pairs perform their tasks first as robots and then as human beings?

– in what ways did their movements change between the two performances?

– why do robots move differently from us?

9 Ask the children to go back into their pairs. This time they must use their machine-like movements to become a *mechanical digger*. One child is the part that digs, and the other the machinery that activates the digger.

10 After the children have had a little time to experiment, put them into larger groups of six to pool ideas and make a more complex machine.

Machines do not dig in silence. The sounds for the children's machines will come from:
- the sounds of the words and phrases in the 'We found' list
- the sound of earth itself and the things we find in it.

Words and phrases

11 Return to the idea of robots. Ask a volunteer to say one of the words or phrases as if a robot were saying it. Ask the robot to repeat the word or phrase several times. Does it sound rhythmical and machine-like?

Ask another child to choose another word or phrase and use it to give a robotic answer to the first robot. This is how machinery works, the movement of one part causing an answering movement from another.

Send the children back to their groups to use words and phrases from the 'We found' list to add sound to their machine movements.

Earth and the things we find in it

12 If we take some fine, dry earth and put it into a tin, it can be shaken to make a sound. Put gravel into the tin and the sound will be different.

Stones can be 'clicked' together.

If we tread in mud, our wellington boots go 'splat' as our feet go in and 'slurp' as we pull them out.

What other earth sounds or earth instruments can the class suggest?

Ask the machine groups to add any appropriate earth sounds to their machines, and ask each group to perform to the class.

13 Now is the time to assemble the complete piece:

IMAGINE   REALITY   IMAGINE

The class will need to make some important decisions:
- how will they manage the transition from the IMAGINE collage into the REALITY section?
- should the REALITY section consist of several mechanical diggers or might they all be linked together to make one enormous earth-moving machine?
- how will the transition back to IMAGINE be contrived?

▶ The transition problem can be solved by continuing the dense background sound while the children move into their positions for the machine(s). To return to IMAGINE, the machines gradually dismantle themselves and go back to the IMAGINE positions. The children continue to make machine sounds and movements until their turn comes to move. Meanwhile those who have reached the IMAGINE positions have started the dense sound. The overlapping sounds cover the *transition*.

Perhaps the children can devise an even better way of doing it.

LISTENING

The Russian composer Igor Stravinsky's revolutionary ballet music *The Rite of Spring* caused riots when it was first performed in Paris in 1913. It is a great celebration of primitive earth-rites.

The last minute of Part I (about fourteen minutes into the piece) is entitled 'Dance of the Earth'. Its powerful repeated rhythms are distinctly machine-like and make good complementary listening to the children's REALITY music.

Immediately afterwards comes the beginning of Part II, 'The Sacrifice'. It begins with dense, slow-moving chords. Explain this density to the children. And do it with complete confidence — you need no musical knowledge to point out:
– the closely-spaced flutes and clarinets at the beginning
– the change of colour to dense oboe, trumpet, and strings sounds (after about thirty seconds when the music suddenly becomes louder).

What other moments in this music do the children feel are dense? They need not explain why.

Do they feel that Stravinsky's dense music is as effective as their own?

PROJECT 2 Air – Sounds and silences

▶ This project needs *space* to be effective. Start it in the school hall or somewhere else where there is room to move around. The idea is to play a number of simple games designed to make the children more aware of space and silence.

Think about air.
Ask the class to sit in *absolute* silence with eyes closed and listen to the air around them. Can the children hear it? If they are outside, they might

hear the sound of air blowing around their ears. If they are indoors, the answer will almost certainly be no. Yet it must be all around us or we wouldn't be here!

What *can* they hear? Ask them to make a mental list of the sounds that come to them through the air—sounds from other classrooms, from outside, from the dinner-ladies.

1 Sounds and silences

Divide the class into four groups and put each group in a corner of the room or hall.

Ask each group in turn to move around its part of the hall with shoes off, disturbing the air as little as possible. Moving fast will disturb the air. So will heads looking around (and mouths opening and closing!).

Ask the rest of the class to listen with eyes closed as each group moves around. Which group can be most silent?

> ▶ Here an element of healthy competition between groups can be a marvellous aid to concentration!

2 Radar

Space the class out around the hall. Everyone must stand in absolute silence whilst one member of the class guides another around the human obstacles by *radar*. The guide emits a continuous beeping sound, the follower is blindfolded.

If the follower touches one of the human obstacles, another pair of children take over (but never the child that the follower bumped into).

3 Circles

Ask half of the class to stand in a large circle in the middle of the hall. Each person must observe exactly where the person opposite them is standing.

Then, with eyes closed, the whole group must walk slowly and carefully across the circle until all of the children think they have reached the place where their opposite number was standing.

If anyone touches anyone else they must glide silently by.

When all movement has stopped, eyes can be opened. How accurate is the new circle?

Now the other half of the class can try.

4 Owai

Sit on the floor in the centre of the hall and ask the class to sit cross-legged in front of you. Imagine you are all in some exotic temple.

Choose two helpers and three instruments that make the most delicate sounds possible.

► If you have three indian bells of different sizes they would be perfect. Or any other really beautiful resonant sound — a glockenspiel note, a *good-quality* triangle (many school triangles can sound appalling) properly suspended on a thin string or thread, etc.

Take one of the instruments yourself and give one to each of your helpers. Ask them to sit on either side of the class.

You and your helpers play *very* occasionally and quite at random, and the class listens with eyes closed. Most of the time there will be silence.

When either of the children plays, the class must silently turn their heads in the direction of the sound. When you play they face the front and murmur the imaginary word 'Owai'.

Ask two more children to choose suitable instruments and to return to their places among the class. Each player must play very sparingly indeed. This time the class simply sits and listens. But when they hear *you* play they may still murmur 'Owai'.

5 Air music

Divide the class into groups of five or six. Ask each group to choose, with the greatest care, sounds that will 'shimmer' through the air without disturbing it, and to invent a piece of *Air music* lasting no longer than forty-five seconds. They may use instruments only, or instruments and voices.

Each group's piece will be mostly air (silence), and the group *must* be able to perform it twice identically.

► The reason behind this rule is that it obliges the children to make precise decisions about their music. They must decide:

- exactly who will play when
- how often each should play
- how long each sound should be
- how much total silence there should be in the piece and where it should come.

LISTENING

When the children have completed this project you might like to play them a tiny piece of music by the Viennese composer Anton Webern.

When composing his *Five Pieces for Orchestra* Op. 10, Webern wrote to his teacher Schoenberg, 'I have already written two orchestral pieces. They are both very brief. Nothing long occurs to me.'* When Webern says brief he means brief! Listen to the first of the *Five Pieces*, written in 1911. Thirty seconds of the most exquisite sounds waft through the air. The fourth piece (originally entitled 'Reminiscence') is even shorter, just twenty seconds.

The children might also enjoy the third piece from *Six Pieces for Orchestra* Op. 6, a comparatively long work at forty seconds!

*Hans Moldenhauer: *Anton Webern* (Gollancz 1978)

PROJECT 3 Fire — Fireworks

▶ This project can be launched by listening to *Fireworks* by Stravinsky, or you may prefer to go straight into the children's work.

LISTENING

In 1908 Stravinsky wrote three and a half minutes of pyrotechnics for orchestra which he called *Fireworks*. Like most composers, he offered no explanation of the music beyond its title. We are free to hear what we will in it.

I hear the lighting of the blue touch-paper at the very beginning, followed by a build-up of sparkling fireworks until the first rocket shoots up through the orchestra (at about 30″). Then (at 50″) a great explosion in the sky, and a gentle cascade of descending coloured lights (the first slow music).

In the middle of the piece (at 1′30″) an expansive melody is accompanied by roman candles, then (at 2′25″) we hear the first banger!

Complete fantasy on my part, but that is the way I hear the music. What do the children see in their own minds?

1 Think about fireworks.

Fireworks

We use fireworks during celebrations to create an exotic display that makes us gasp with surprise and pleasure. Some fireworks are purely visual — roman candles delight us with their colours, sparklers with a vivid texture of sparks. Others, like bangers, are designed to make us jump. Some of the more expensive fireworks do both.

This project draws parallels between what we see and what we hear. Quite often we hear a piece of music that reminds us of something we have seen. And we can also see things that remind us of a piece of music.

2 Roman candle or sparkler?

Take a *metallophone* and seat four children around it (two on either side), each armed with two soft beaters. Ask the children to choose two notes each and to play their notes all together, quickly, and as quietly as possible.

Now seat four more children around a *glockenspiel*, this time with hard beaters. Ask them to play in the same way.

One group is the warm glow of a *roman candle*, and the other is a *sparkler*. Which does the class think is which?

▶ In music we frequently borrow words from the vocabulary we normally use to describe visual and tactile sensations and use them to describe qualities of sound. Hence we might use the word 'smooth' to describe the warm, sustained sound produced on a metallophone, and we might describe the glockenspiel as 'sparkling'. Professional musicians use these words in exactly the same way as the layman.

3 Take the experiment a little further. Could the metallophone group find a way of making their roman candle start gradually, build up into a bright glow, and then fade away again?

▶ There are a number of ways of achieving this effect:
— start very softly, get louder, and then get softer again
— start with one player alone, add players, then subtract them again
— or the children may find some other way of doing it — there are no right ways or wrong ways.

4 Would the group like to add the sound of the striking match and the fizzing of the touch-paper? They can choose different instruments for this if they wish.

Can one of the children suggest a way of making the musical roman candle change colour?

▶ 'Colour' is a word that musicians use frequently. We say that the sound of a metallophone is a different 'colour' from the sound of a glockenspiel (or indeed any other instrument). However, it is not necessary to change instruments to change colour. A change of beaters on an instrument should result in a change of colour, harder beaters giving a brighter sound and softer beaters a more mellow sound.

5 Tom & Jerry and Laurel & Hardy have ensured that children are familiar with the relationship between a descending scale of notes and someone falling downstairs! If you were to light the blue touch-paper:
– could one of the children make a musical rocket shoot up into the air?
– could someone else produce a mid-air explosion?
– could the group then create a cascade of beautiful colours floating back to earth?

6 Divide the class into groups of six and ask each group either to invent its *own* firework or a specific firework suggested by you.

7 When each group has performed its firework, discuss ways in which the whole class could use their fireworks to create a *musical firework display*. The children will have to decide on a shape for their display:
– should it start quietly or with a flourish?
– should each firework have its own chance to shine alone or should fireworks overlap?
– should the display increase in excitement as it progresses? If so, how can this be achieved?
– how should the display finish?

   In the middle of his firework display, Stravinsky introduces a melody which threads its way through the glowing fireworks. This has the effect of tying the music together with a continuous strand of sound. Would it be effective if someone played or sang a tune ('Boys and girls come out to play' might be suitable) or better still if somebody *invented* a tune to tie the whole display together?

PROJECT 4 Water — Cataclysm Part I

▶ This project combines music and movement. As some of the children will be involved in creating music while others invent movement or dance, you may find it more practical to work with the whole class on both aspects simultaneously.

You will need space to move about — the school hall would be an ideal working area.

The piece, *Cataclysm*, is quite long, so I have divided it into two parts (Projects 4 and 5) which can be tackled in separate lessons.

Think about water.

Water covers seventy per cent of our planet. In its liquid form it splashes, it sloshes about, it makes us wet.

But it can take other forms. Think about what happens to the sea as we go towards the north or south pole, and what happens to water in the proximity of a volcano.

This project could grow out of a science lesson.

Heat up an ice cube in front of the class and ask the children to observe *exactly* what happens. Did the class notice that early in the process there was both ice and water in the container?

Then the water turned to steam; not all at once but by a gradual process of *transformation*.

And that is what this project is about — the *transformation* of sound and movement.

▶ The ability to make one musical idea grow out of or into another is one of the basic skills of handling musical material. At the end of this project I suggest examples of this process from Beethoven, Dvořák and Holst for the children to listen to.

Cataclysm Part I

66 *You are on a frozen planet. Everything is stiff and motionless. The only impression of movement is the glinting of light from a distant sun catching one frozen shape and then another.* 99

1 Can the class capture the eerie stillness of the place? Perhaps the children should stand, lie, or crouch in frozen positions, making grotesque shapes on the landscape.

2 Could some of the frozen figures choose small instruments to make glints of sound as the light catches the ice? The sounds must be icy cold.
What sort of sounds do the children find really chilly?

▶ You may already have discussed cold sounds in the 'Winter' project (**The seasons**, Project 2). I personally find ringing high-pitched metallic sounds cold (an Indian bell struck with a metal beater for instance). But the important thing is what the children think.

How could we give the impression of the light striking first one spot, then another, over a vast frozen landscape? Would the effect be better if we made frequent or occasional sounds?

66 *But the distant sun is dying. Slowly, over millions of years it expands, and slowly the temperature on the frozen planet rises. The ice begins to melt. Soon pools of water appear, spreading and spreading until the entire surface of the planet is covered with water.* 99

3 How gradually can the children unfreeze from their grotesque positions? Should their first tiny movements be stiff, only gradually becoming more fluid? The process takes millions of years!
What sort of movement would be appropriate as the children turn into water? Should they move from one place to another or remain fixed?

▶ When the children have decided on the sort of movements they would like to make as they turn from ice to water, it might be a good idea to sit them down to discuss the next stage in the musical side of the project.

4 How can we produce sounds that *flow* like water? We can certainly make our voices flow—smooth continuous singing flows.

Perhaps we could use instruments. Playing a wind instrument is very like singing: we control the sound with our breath. If you have recorder players in the class, ask one of them to start on one note and to flow smoothly from it to another note. The process should be done in one continuous breath. Now flow onto a third and then a fourth note, still in one breath. Do we get a flowing effect if the player repeats this little phrase again and again, playing smoothly and slowly?

What sort of *rhythm* flows best, a smooth one or a jerky one?

▶ If you have a group of recorder players, send them away to elaborate this idea. They must decide whether they should all play the same thing or whether it would work well if each invented something different.

5 Explore another idea with the rest of the class. Could we create flowing sounds on a metallophone or xylophone?

Ask a child to invent a fragment of melody that always moves between *adjacent* notes. No leaps are allowed. How does it sound if the player weaves a line of notes, sometimes going for several notes in the same direction, sometimes turning back and changing direction?

▶ If you have a metallophone, this exercise will produce a flowing line of notes. A metallophone is extremely resonant and one note will blur into the next. On a xylophone the effect will be quite different. Here there is an almost total lack of reverberation.

Would it sound more appropriate if the beaters were swished up and down the xylophone so that no note was actually struck?

This might be more suitable as a background texture than as a foreground idea. It could be used to accompany the recorders. Do the children like the idea?

Are there any other instruments that can produce flowing music?

6 Now we must solve an important problem. Whilst the dancers (for that is what they really are) gradually unfreeze, the musicians must find a way of making a smooth transition from glinting icy sounds to flowing watery music.

▶ The glinting sounds are short and isolated. The flowing sounds are continuous. One solution is for the glinting sounds to become more frequent as the ice melts. The flowing instruments can join in very quietly, first with isolated notes, then joining two notes together, then three as they begin to flow. And the glinting sounds get softer and softer until they disappear.

What is the children's solution to this problem? Give the musicians a chance to practise this *metamorphosis* while the dancers practise unfreezing and flowing.

7 Perform the project from the beginning. The dancers must always *listen* to the musicians, and the musicians must *watch* the dancers. Only in this way can the music and the movement be made to match one another.

PROJECT 5 Cataclysm Part II

1 Perform Cataclysm Part I to refresh the children's memories. Then read on.

> 66 *The sun has grown to a gigantic size. Great explosions throw flares thousands of miles out into space. The water on the planet no longer flows. It bubbles and froths as it begins to boil.* 99

2 The movements of the dancers have been relaxed and flowing. Now they must transform themselves into a bubbling cauldron. How can this best be achieved?

Would rapid movement (like rushing around the hall) be effective? Or should they cluster together in a seething mass?

▶ Try out both possibilities, and any others the children suggest, and let the class decide what works best as a group movement.

3 Now that we know how we are going to act as a group, we must decide on our own individual movements. What sort of movements 'bubble'?

4 The music must bubble too. Not suddenly, but gradually, like a pan of water coming to the boil — first one or two bubbles, then more and more until the whole surface bubbles.

Can anyone suggest a way of making instruments bubble? Try out a few ideas.

▶ Recorders can be made to bubble in a number of ways. Rapid random movement of all fingers may work. Or trilling, moving one finger up and down. Try also rolling an 'r' or gargling in the throat whilst blowing. (This is a standard technique of wind-playing called 'flutter-tonguing'.)

What about metallophones and xylophones as bubbling instruments?

5 In Part II, rather than the same children being dancers and musicians throughout the piece, it might be fairer (and more interesting) for the water-dancers of Part I to flow one by one to instruments and begin to play bubbling music, freeing the musicians to become boiling dancers.

> ▶ Give the two groups of children a chance to practise the boiling dance and the bubbling music separately. Then practise the changeover between Parts I and II. If this becomes too efficient the music and dance will change character suddenly! What we want is a *gradual transformation.*

" *With a cataclysmic explosion the supernova bursts, spraying debris millions of miles into space in all directions. The planet is vaporized instantly.* **"**

6 There is nothing gradual about the ending! It happens in a flash.

Discuss how this might be achieved. Perhaps the bubbling should get louder and more concentrated. Could we use voices to intensify the atmosphere of impending drama?

How can we create a cataclysmic explosion? Could every person contribute to the sound?

How can the whole scene be made to evaporate?

7 Practise the ending then prepare to perform the whole piece from the beginning.

> ▶ Before trying a complete performance some practical suggestions. The project works well if the water instruments are placed in the centre of the hall. Start with the whole class in frozen positions around the hall, musicians with 'cold' instruments in hands. As they thaw the water musicians move to the instruments in the centre. When the water boils, musicians and dancers cluster tightly in the centre, then explode to all sides of the hall.

Remind the children again how important it is that everyone listens and watches as they perform. Then perform *Cataclysm.*

LISTENING

During Projects 4 and 5, I emphasized the process of moving gradually from one musical idea to another. This way of developing ideas was reflected in the movements we invented.

Listen to the beginning of the last movement of Beethoven's First Symphony. It is an excellent example of a composer working his way gradually into an idea, so that it doesn't start suddenly. First he writes three notes and pauses. Then four, then five, and so on until he has built a complete scale of notes which floats into the movement itself.

If you decide to play the complete movement to the children, ask them to look out for this scale and identify (perhaps by putting up their hands) each time it comes. It is a great help to us all to have something to look out for when we listen to a piece of music for the first time.

Dvořák is a master at sliding out of one idea and into another with no perceptible join. Listen to the opening of the famous slow movement from the 'New World' Symphony. It starts with sombre brass chords, then one of the best-loved tunes ever invented, played on the cor anglais.

Now jump to the end of the movement where this tune comes back, and listen to the way Dvořák winds the movement down. The famous tune is played as at the beginning, on the cor anglais. The strings take it over, hesitating three times and, as it is finally laid to rest by the wind section, Dvořák weaves a gentle thread of violins that drifts back into the brass chords that opened the movement, rounding it off perfectly.

'Mercury the Winged Messenger', the third piece from *The Planets* by Gustav Holst, is constructed from three very different ingredients—a wispy impression of the 'Winged Messenger' (the beginning), a series of descending wind chords ending with a bounce (after about twenty-seven seconds, starting just after the solo violin starts playing morse code—a reference to another sort of winged message) and a section of smooth melody (after about fifty-three seconds) which always moves to adjacent notes and repeats itself over and over again (a good example of flowing melody).

Listen to how skilfully Holst moves between these three ideas, never directly from one to another, always giving a foretaste of the idea to come before launching into it, so that the transition is as smooth as possible.

Play the piece to the children two or three times so that they get to know it. Then get them to put their hands up each time they hear the first hint that Holst is about to move from one musical idea to the next.

CHAPTER SEVEN

Just imagine . . .

THIS CHAPTER IS ABOUT:

Creating atmosphere
Musical colour and physical dexterity
Drones and rhythmic dance music
Musical structure.

This final chapter is based on the Russian legend of the Firebird. It is designed to enable you to draw together some of the strands from earlier chapters of the book, should you wish to do so.

The projects can be used:
— as four separate music projects
— as a sequence of scenes to make a complete tableau
— as music and drama/mime projects
— as music and dance projects.

The chapter is inspired by Igor Stravinsky's ballet music, *The Firebird*, which was first performed in Paris in 1910. Each project borrows a musical idea from Stravinsky for the children to use in their work, and at the end of each project I have given a guide to appropriate listening from Stravinsky's music.

▶   It is important to emphasize that it is not my intention that the children should mimic the music of Stravinsky, but rather that they should produce their own original work and then have the opportunity of hearing what Stravinsky made of a similar task. I therefore strongly advocate that the children complete each project *before* listening to *The Firebird*.

PROJECT 1 The deadly forest

▶   This project is about creating atmosphere and using short sections of music that repeat again and again.

I like to tackle it by first exploring each element of the scenario with the class, then dividing into groups and assigning one element to each group. Finally the class is brought together to assemble the complete scenario.

Before you start, set up two xylophones or metallophones taking off all the bars except:

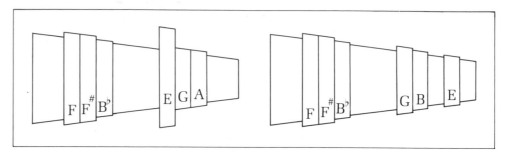

 A child is lost in a forest. The forest is a very dangerous place indeed. Many people from the nearby town have entered it but few have ever returned. Nobody knows why this is.

1 Think about fear.

What do people feel like when they are really afraid? Some people go hot, some go cold, some shake, some speak very quickly.

How do animals behave when they are afraid? Why do creatures adopt a different mode of behaviour when they are afraid?

This project might grow out of a science lesson. You could tell the children about adrenalin and the way the human body copes with stress.

How do the children imagine someone alone in the forest described above would behave?
– would they stand upright or crouch?
– would they make a lot of noise or would they creep along?

2 Use the notes illustrated above on the two xylophones to make music for somebody creeping through a forest. Ask four children to come and play them to the class. Each child plays three notes: softly, evenly, and quite slowly. The children play one after the other without pausing.

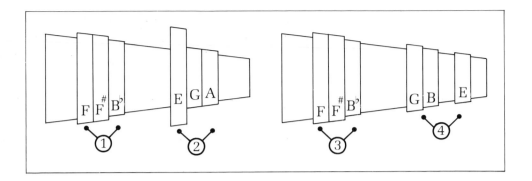

Ask them to try it first this way:
Child 1 plays right to left (B♭, F♯, F) then
Child 2 left to right (E, G, A)
Child 3 right to left and back (B♭, F♯, B♭)
Child 4 left to right (G, B, E)
When they have got the knack of it ask them to play the whole sequence through four times.

3 How would it sound if the children played in a different order?
– can someone in the class suggest a new order?
– does the phrase sound effective played with evenly spaced notes or should a more varied rhythm be adopted?

4 Can one other person join the group of four and choose a new sound that will make the music more *sinister*?

▶   A soft roll on a drum might be effective. Or the continuous rattle of a tambourine being shaken. Or a maraca.

What does the class suggest?

66 *After a while, the frightened child stops and listens. All that can be heard is the rustling of small animals in the undergrowth. Even these sound terrifying.* **99**

5 The 'creeping' music stops here. How might we create music that suggests the sounds of small animals in the undergrowth of a dark forest? Ask the children to choose some sounds that might conjure up different unseen creatures.

▶   The brief rattle of castanets, the scrape of a guiro, the sudden wail of a recorder mouthpiece might all be suitable.

– how often should each person play?
– would the sounds be more effective against a background of silence or of continuous rustling?

Ask the children to try both possibilities. Perhaps they could vote on which is more effective.

❝ *The terrified child creeps on.* **❞**

6 When the class assembles the complete piece this might be the place for the xylophones (or whichever instruments have been chosen) to start playing again. The children will have to decide whether to play their notes in the same order as before, or whether to try a new note-order.

❝ *Again the child stops. The wind sighs eerily in the branches of the trees.* **❞**

7 For this part of the scenario our mouths may be by far the best instruments. It can, however, be quite difficult to make whistling and whooshing sounds *really* frightening. Can the children think of any other ways of making eerie wind sounds?

> ► Blowing across bottles or running fingers around the rims of wine glasses might be effective (but beware broken glass!). Blowing half into, half across plastic gutter fall-pipe or cardboard tubing with the edge resting on the chin can be extraordinarily evocative. Or perhaps orthodox instruments can be used in unorthodox ways.

What can the children devise?

❝ *As the dusk deepens the child creeps on. In the distance a wolf howls. The exhausted child collapses against a rotting tree-stump and gazes into the gloom, shivering with helpless terror.* **❞**

Children have no difficulty with wolf-howls!
– how could this one be made to seem distant?
– how might the child's shiver be achieved?
– should these sounds be heard against a background of other sounds?

8 Divide the class into groups and assign a task to each group.
Group 1: to decide on an order or orders of notes for the creeping music, and a background to accompany it.
Group 2: to invent an effective scene using the sounds of small animals.
Group 3: to produce wind in the trees that will chill the listener to the bone.
Group 4: to find a wolf, a shiver, and an atmosphere that will draw the scene to a satisfactory close.

▶ If you wish, these tasks could be allotted to groups of children with mixed abilities. The task for group 1 could stretch the more able child while group 2 might be ideal for children with learning difficulties.

Allow each group to show its completed work to the class.

9 Then help the class to assemble the complete scenario. Is it more effective with a narrator reading the text or as a continuous piece of evocative music?

LISTENING

In 1919 Stravinsky extracted six sections from his ballet music, *The Firebird*, to be performed as a suite in the concert hall. I recommend that you listen to this 1919 version rather than trying to locate the relevant passages in the complete ballet music.

The suite opens with the 'creeping melody' that you set up at the beginning of the project (although Stravinsky opts to write the phrase at a lower pitch). It is played by violas, cellos, and double basses against the background of a soft bass drum roll. Before long the trombones add a sinister counterpoint.

What I have chosen to interpret as small animals in the undergrowth are twitching sounds from clarinets, bassoons, and trumpets (after about 50″). The background is silence.

The creeping music returns; then more creatures in the undergrowth.

A sudden loud note from the horn, the strings shudder, and the wind sighs eerily in the trees (about 1′40″). This extraordinary effect is achieved by asking all the string players (except the basses) to slide their fingers very lightly up and down a string while bowing their instruments very softly. What we hear are called 'harmonic' notes.

The creeping music returns for a last time.

After five drum notes, a distant wolf (horn) howls. Strings shiver and the piano shudders—a swift flicker of notes (sometimes played instead on the celeste, a sort of metallophone with a piano keyboard). Then Stravinsky's music runs straight into the next project.

PROJECT 2 **The Firebird**

▶ This project is about musical colour and physical dexterity.

In my version of the story, the Firebird is the most important character. It is the Firebird that protects the child and defeats the evil magician whom we shall meet in Project 3.

1 Start this project with a game.

Place four or five tuned percussion instruments (e.g., a xylophone, two glockenspiels, a metallophone, a series of chime bars) in a circle on the floor. Ask for four or five volunteers, and give each a pair of beaters.

▶ If you are short of tuned percussion, ask the children to sit two to an instrument, one playing the high notes, one the low notes.

The game is simple. You count seconds out loud, and each child in succession plays as many random notes as realistically possible for 1 second. The children must follow one another without a break so the game will take a mere 4 or 5 seconds to play.

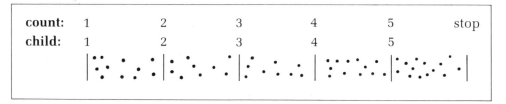

count:	1	2	3	4	5	stop
child:	1	2	3	4	5	

▶ I say as many notes as 'realistically possible' because if the players try to play too fast or too loudly their arms will seize up. Give them a few seconds to practise playing *quite* fast with very relaxed arms.

Let the children play the game two or three times. When they have got the hang of it and the sound is continuous, see if they can do it without you counting.

Send the children back to their seats, and let some more teams of volunteers have a go.

2 At some appropriate point, add another element to the game. To finish, each child must play again, this time running a beater the full length of the instrument. This sound, too, must be continuous, like this:

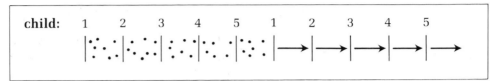

Try this with one or two groups, then add a last dimension.

3 Ask for two more volunteers and arm one with a maraca and the other with a triangle. Now the rules get more complicated. The children play their fast notes one after the other. When the child shakes the maraca they stop. The maraca can be played for a short while or a long while. As soon as the maraca stops, the children start again where they left off. Only when the triangle plays do they move onto their final sweep up the instrument.

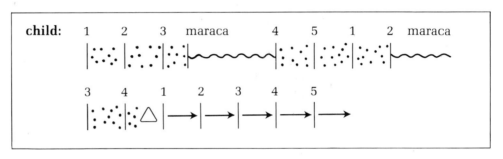

▶ If you wish to stretch some of the children a little further, you might suggest:
  – that some of the one-second bursts could be elongated to make the music less predictable. This will, however, increase the difficulty of achieving a fluent performance.
  – that instead of playing random notes, each child should decide on a precise group of notes, and play the same notes each time they perform.

4 When every child has had a go at one or other of the tasks, read the scenario to the class.

66 *Suddenly the Firebird bursts into sight. The entire forest is lit up by the brilliant colours of its wings as it swoops and darts among the trees.* 99

Play this Firebird game with the class. The whole class stands motionless. Each child is a tree. Then one child comes alive and swoops in and out among the trees. After a few seconds, the Firebird child touches one of the trees who in turn becomes the Firebird. The first child returns to being a tree.

▶ The rapid succession of children, each briefly becoming the Firebird, represents the speed of the Firebird 'deceiving the eye'. And each different child represents a different colour on the Firebird's wings.

Point out to the class that this game is very like the musical game they have just played on the instruments.

5 Explain musical 'colour' to the children.

▶ See **Miniatures**, Project 2, and **The elements**, Project 3 where colour in music was discussed in detail.

The game we have just played was designed to capture the impression of the exotic Firebird darting among the trees. By using different tuned percussion instruments we have already achieved a *multicoloured* texture.

6 Divide into groups. These may contain as many as ten children if they wish to use more than two 'stopping' instruments (like the maraca and the triangle).

▶ Even with children doubling-up on tuned percussion, you may run into the problem of a shortage of instruments. Of course, recorders, orchestral instruments, and keyboards may be used for the fast-note clusters. Another solution may be to send some children away to create their music, while the rest of the class concentrates on movement/dance.

▶ Then, as in Project 1, make sure all the children have a chance to make music and to dance at some stage.

7 The finished Firebird scene can be wonderfully effective when performed in the most colourful costumes the children can contrive.

LISTENING

In the 1919 suite, the 'Firebird's Dance' follows the opening music without pause. The strings tremble with excitement, the initial swoop of fast wind and string notes is followed by a brief silence, then the dance proper begins.

Stravinsky achieves the multicoloured darting effect in the simplest possible way (though not for the musicians—the dance is extremely difficult to play!). Players are thrust into the limelight playing short showers of notes; first the clarinets and flutes, then the strings. As in the children's game, no individual remains prominent for more than a split second.

There is, of course, nothing random about Stravinsky's music. He found composition a long, difficult task, thinking out and writing down every note with painstaking precision. So each successive performance sounds identical.

PROJECT 3 Kastchei's Dance

This project is about drones and rhythmic dance music.

LISTENING

You might start this project by listening to some music that uses a *drone* as an accompaniment. Perhaps you can find a recording of the Scottish bagpipes or some dance music played on the Irish uilleann pipes (pronounced 'eelun'). The Northumbrian pipes and the Scottish small pipes (blown in the same way as the uilleann pipes—by a bellows strapped under the player's right arm)

all produce drone notes to accompany the melodies played on them.

Or you might decide to turn to the classics and listen to the opening of the last movement of Haydn's 104th Symphony (the 'London' symphony), the 'Pastorale' from Handel's *Messiah*, or the 'Arab Dance' from Tchaikovsky's *Nutcracker Suite*. All three composers use a drone, or continuously sounded note, as an accompaniment to sections of these pieces of music.

Listen to the 'Gavotte and Musette' from Grieg's *Holberg Suite*. Can the children put their hands up every time a section using a drone is heard?

Drones

Drones are one of the most ancient forms of musical accompaniment. Bagpipes have existed in cultures throughout the world for many hundreds of years. Other instruments (string instruments and the didgeridoo, to give two diverse examples) are used to play drone accompaniments, often with a pulsed drone i.e., a repeated note rather than a continuous sound.

---

1 Experiment with drones.

Sing a round with the class ('London's burning' and 'Frère Jacques' are ideal). But instead of singing them as rounds, ask half of the class to take a deep breath and hang onto the first note while the rest of the class sings the complete song.

2 Now take a rest from drones and play a game with the class.

Clap a steady pulse (slightly slower than two claps to a second should work well) and wander round the classroom. When you stop in front of a particular child, the child must clap a simple rhythm over your pulse (see **Pulse and Rhythm**, Project 1) while you continue to clap. For example:

You	• •
child 1	• • •• ••
child 2	• • • •• •

▶ Be careful not to let children feel that they have 'failed' in a game like this. I say 'Good' and move on after a second or two, *whatever* a child claps. Soon the children gain confidence from one another and the 'success' rate improves dramatically. I *never* say 'No, you're wrong!'

3 Now set up a xylophone, isolating the three notes E, F♯, and G.

▶ These are adjacent notes, so simply take a bar away from either side of them, but do remember to substitute F♯ for F.

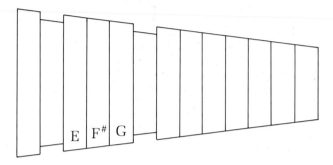

Play the clapping game again. This time, instead of clapping, each child must come out and play his or her rhythm using the three xylophone notes in any order to form a short musical phrase.

4 Set up another xylophone (or similar instrument) with the same three notes plus two more, B♭ and B:

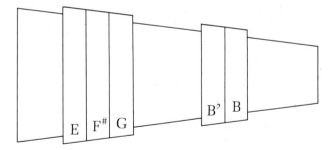

Ask a volunteer to invent a phrase using these five notes and the rhythm he or she clapped to you.

Ask the children to make a musical 'sandwich' out of their two phrases, one using the three notes and the other using five.

child 1   child 2   child 1

5 Now is the time to tell the class about Kastchei, the evil magician.

❝ *Kastchei searches out people who get lost in the forest, turns them to stone and uses them as ornaments in the garden of his castle.* ❞

6 The notes and rhythms that we have been inventing in the game will form the basis of 'Kastchei's Dance'.

The dance is accompanied by a drone. Would this drone sound more fearsome as a single, sustained note, or as a repeated pulse or rhythm?

Ask someone to choose a suitable instrument for whichever of these two options is preferred and to perform the drone using the note E.

▶ If a keyboard has been chosen, E is the white note lying immediately to the right of each of the *pairs* of black notes (see Glossary, p. 121).

Add the musical 'sandwich' on top of the drone E. Would it be more effective if a deep or a high E were used?

7 Discuss ways of extending the sandwich idea by adding *untuned percussion interludes*. Draw up a plan for discussion on the board:

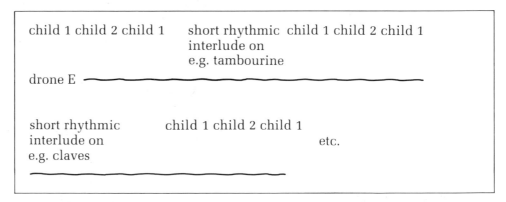

child 1 child 2 child 1   short rhythmic   child 1 child 2 child 1
                    interlude on
                    e.g. tambourine

drone E ——————————————————————————

short rhythmic   child 1 child 2 child 1
interlude on   etc.
e.g. claves

——————————————————

8 Divide into groups of six to invent a savage dance with rhythmic interludes.

▶ As in the previous project, recorders, violins, etc., can take the place of xylophones. And two children can still share one xylophone, sitting on either side of it:

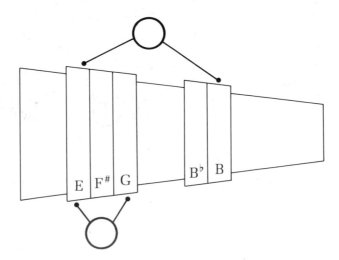

▶ You may even wish to extend the xylophone idea one stage further by adding another two notes to make a group of seven available. Add C♯ and D:

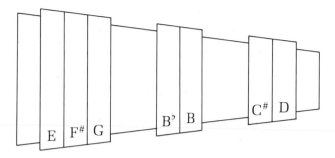

9 When the groups have finished work, ask each to perform to the class. And after the performances you may like to discuss ways of joining up the group pieces to make one large dance. Here is another plan for discussion:

xylophone children group 1	interlude all metal percussion	xylophone children group 2	interlude all wooden percussion	etc.

all drones ⎯⎯⎯⎯⎯⎯⎯⎯⎯⎯⎯⎯⎯⎯⎯⎯⎯⎯⎯⎯⎯⎯

LISTENING

The notes I chose for the xylophones are those chosen by Stravinsky for his 'Kastchei's Dance', the fourth movement of the suite. Stravinsky's drone is played with terrifying speed on timpani and double basses. Rather than using percussion instruments for his interludes, Stravinsky invents new melodies — but he is a little more advanced than we are! Nevertheless, like the children's pieces, his opening idea comes back again and again. Here is another opportunity for the children to discover Stravinsky's musical structure as they listen to the music.

Play the very beginning of the movement two or three times so that the children become familiar with it (it is extraordinarily memorable). Then play the complete dance, asking the children to indicate in some way every time the opening block of music occurs. I find this sort of positive listening a great aid to concentration.

The 'Dance' ends in a great swirl of instruments. You can easily imagine Kastchei disappearing in a flash and a puff of smoke!

CHAPTER SEVEN **Just imagine**

PROJECT 4 Awakening and celebration

This project is about drones and layers of sounds. If you have decided to make a tableau out of the four projects, the children might well wish to finish their 'Kastchei's Dance' in a similar way to Stravinsky. For this is how Kastchei does indeed disappear.

> 66 *Kastchei is vanquished by the Firebird, disappears in a puff of smoke, and almost immediately the stone statues in his garden begin to come alive.*
>
> *When the missing people return to the town there are great celebrations.* 99

1 Discuss celebration.
Imagine the scene when the missing people return to the town. No doubt individual families and friends would celebrate in their own ways. But when a whole town celebrates every joyful sound is used, and perhaps most of all the ringing of church bells.

2 Ask five children to be bell-ringers. Give each child a chime bar and a beater and ask them to play the peal of bells in the diagram. The bars are numbered in order of playing:

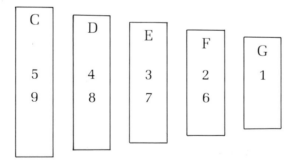

Have the children listened to church bells being rung? In theory, they ring out one after the other in a stately peal. In practice the co-ordination is not always perfect.
Now the children know why!

3 To add strength to the sound ask a volunteer to underpin the peal with a drone; play a long G. The effect will be strongest if the G is a fairly low note:
 – the lowest G on a keyboard

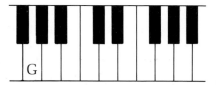

 – the G string of a cello (if you have one in the class)
 – the lowest string of a violin
 – a fairly low G on a piano (reiterated as the sound dies away).

4 Explain the sequence of notes in the peal to the rest of the class. It might help to draw the diagram on the board. Can one person come out and play the whole peal on a xylophone starting on G?

Then ask the xylophone player to play the same *shape* starting on any note *except* G.

▶ The child will be playing in parallel to the bell-ringers. If he or she starts on E, for example:

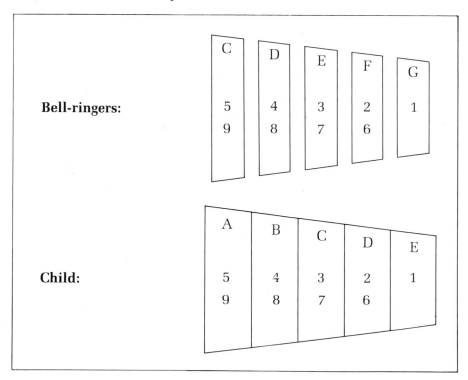

The effect of chime bars and xylophone together will be quite different each time the xylophone player starts on a new note. Ask the player to try two or three different starting notes. Which version does the class prefer?

5 Ask someone else to choose an instrument—a xylophone, keyboard, or glockenspiel—and to add another layer, starting on yet another note.

> ▶ The sound of a bell is acoustically complex. Bells sound as they do because in what seems to be a single note our ears are in fact able to detect a number of different notes competing very strongly with one another.
>
> What the children are doing in this part of the project is constructing a complex block of sound for each 'bell' note.

6 How does it sound if someone else adds another layer by playing a 'mirror shape' to the chime bar players, i.e., going upwards instead of downwards?

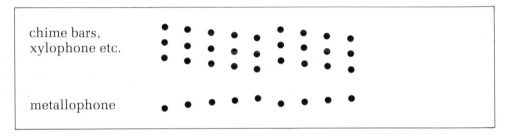

chime bars,
xylophone etc.

metallophone

– which starting note should we choose for this 'mirror shape'? Give the children a chance to experiment, starting on different notes. Then perhaps the children could vote on which version they like best.
– could another layer be added to this *rising* shape?

7 Ask the children to repeat their bell music four times. Could somebody choose an *important sound* to mark the beginning of each repeat of the phrase?

> ▶ A gong or a cymbal with their impressive resonance might be suitable. What do the children think?

8 If we repeat a phrase again and again it will soon lose its appeal. If we alter the drone note, however, the other notes are thrown into a completely new perspective.
Try this out by changing the drone note to C. How does that sound?
Are there any other drone notes we can find that will work well with the bell music? Perhaps we could play the peal four times with a new drone note, and then return to the original G.

9 Ask one group of children (it may be as many as ten) to go away and practise the bell music.

10 Now the rest of the class can act out the waking of Kastchei's victims.
Spread the children around the room as statues. They will have to stand motionless, so perhaps it would be as well not to adopt potentially uncomfortable poses!
Would one member of the class volunteer to play a sustained C drone (perhaps on a keyboard) that will last for the whole scene? It might be effective if all the statues were to *hum* this note quietly as well.

11 Then one at a time, ask each child to 'come alive'.
As each person begins to move, he or she must make a new sustained sound. It could be a hummed note different from the drone C, or it may come from an instrument that the statue is already holding—a maraca, sleigh bells, a mouth-organ. It must be very quiet indeed.
As more and more statues come to life the sound will become denser (but not a lot louder).

12 Would it be effective if one child played the descending bell peal slowly and quietly, perhaps on the low notes of a recorder, again and again as the statues come alive? Should others join in as the awakening progresses?

Bring back the group working on the bell music ready for the finale.

13 When all of the statues have come back to life and the sounds are at their most intense, the drone can change to G and the bell-players can burst in with joyful celebration. Or would the children prefer some other way of bringing the scene to its climax?
Should the statue children adopt a pose symbolic of celebration as the bells ring out, or should they celebrate with joyous movement?

LISTENING

The final scene of Stravinsky's *Firebird* adopts the same dramatic shape as our project.

The music opens with the notes of our bell phrase played on a solo horn. Stravinsky varies the shape of the phrase a little:

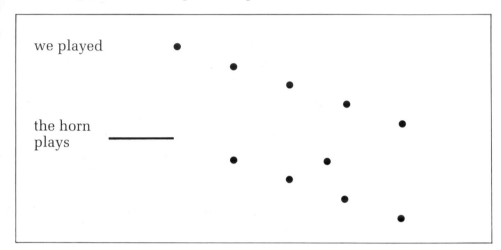

i.e., making the first note longer and dodging back to the first note between notes three and four.

He varies the second part of the phrase in a similar way, but the feel of the music is the same.

This is the beginning of his waking up music. It is accompanied by shimmering strings.

As more and more statues come to life, more players join the melody until the whole orchestra is playing the phrase (except the double basses, tuba, and timpani who play the drone).

Then, after a brief flurry of excitement from the strings, the same melody is transformed into a triumphant peal of bells, played first by trumpets and trombones.

The music ends with a series of magnificent brass chords.

Glossary of terms used in the text

accompaniment
the background sounds which play a supporting role to a tune or some other important sound.

autoharp
a modern zither with wires stretched across a hollow resonating box.
When a button is pressed, a bar descends and damps off specific wires so that the remaining wires make a chord when they are strummed. Another button and bar makes another chord, and so on.

B
if you have a xylophone, metallophone or glockenspiel made in Germany, the note sounding B♭ will be engraved with the letter B (see H).

ballet music
music specially composed so that a choreographer can create a ballet to it.

bass
low; applied to instruments (e.g., bass tuba), voices (e.g., a bass singer), and sounds (e.g., the bass notes of the piano).

beat
the steady pulse (to which we tap our feet) that underlies a rhythmic piece of music. We say that a conductor beats time — he is simply beating out this pulse.

beaters
the sound of a percussion instrument can be altered considerably by using different beaters (e.g., hard rubber beaters or soft felt beaters on a xylophone). Experiment to find out what is most effective.
Beaters must be allowed to bounce off xylophones, glockenspiels, chime bars, etc., after impact. The correct way to hold them is:

 *not*

bend-wheel
a wheel on an electric keyboard that allows the player to alter the pitch of a note – turn the wheel away from you and the note "bends" upwards, towards you and it bends downwards.

brass section
the group of metal instruments in an orchestra blown by vibrating the lips against a cup-shaped mouthpiece, and consisting of trumpets, cornets, French horns, trombones, tubas. Sometimes joined by Wagner tubas (e.g., in Stravinsky's *The Rite of Spring* — see **The elements**, Project 1, p. 87) and the euphonium, a small tuba (e.g., in Holst's *The Planets* — see **Opposites and contrasts**, Project 3, p. 49).

121

bridge

the piece of wood that serves the dual purpose of holding the strings away from the belly of a string instrument and of carrying the vibrations of the strings into the resonating body of the instrument.

celeste

see **Just imagine**, Project 1, p. 107.

chord

three or more notes sounded simultaneously.

colour

see **Miniatures**, Project 2, p. 14; **The elements**, Project 3, p. 94.

counterpoint

the playing of two or more melodies simultaneously or, in the case of a round (q.v.), the same melody with each part starting at a different time.

didgeridoo

a straight, hollowed tree-branch blown in the same way as a brass instrument (but without a mouth-piece), and producing a single, deep continuous note. The instrument is unique to the Australian aboriginal people who produce the continuous sound by circular breathing — compressing the cheeks whilst snatching breath through the nose.

drone

a continuous or continuously repeated note serving as accompaniment to a melody (e.g., on the bagpipes).

drum roll

see 'roll'.

flat (♭)

see 'Where the notes are to be found on a keyboard'.

gavotte

an old French dance of moderate speed (often associated with a musette, q.v.).

glockenspiel

like a xylophone but with thin *metal* bars. The xylophone has wooden bars.

graphic notation

an approximate way of writing down music using invented symbols to represent the required sounds on paper.

guiro

a wooden, torpedo-like percussion instrument with serrations on the surface. Played by scraping a wooden stick over the serrated edge.

H

if you have a xylophone, glockenspiel or metallophone made in Germany, the note sounding B will be engraved with the letter H (see B).

harmonics

high, ethereal-sounding notes produced on string instruments by touching the string lightly with a finger at a specific point whilst drawing the bow across the string. On brass or wind instruments, the series of natural notes that can be produced from a tube by blowing progressively harder or by pursing the lips more tightly. Harmonics are the only notes that can be produced on a bugle (as it has no valves), and they are the notes that make up all the tunes played on bugles by Boy Scout and Boys Brigade bands.

Indian bells/finger cymbals
tiny cymbals that may either be struck together edge-on or with a metal beater.

marimba
a large xylophone with resonator tubes under each bar. Used to wonderful effect in modern jazz as well as in contemporary music.

metallophone
a large glockenspiel with heavy metal bars.

movement
some longer musical works (e.g., symphonies, suites, q.v.) consist of several self-contained pieces of music. These are usually called 'movements'.

musette
an old French dance which imitates the bagpipes and is accompanied by a drone. It is often found in association with a gavotte (q.v.), the pair of dances being performed: gavotte — musette — gavotte.

Northumbrian pipes
small bagpipes blown by a bellows strapped under the player's right arm.

op./opus
Latin word meaning 'a work'. The first piece of music written by a composer is called 'opus 1', the second 'opus 2', etc.

panpipes
a series of graduated bamboo tubes bound together in a line and blown over the end of each tube. Most frequently heard in music from South America.

pastorale
a gentle piece of music (originally a dance), perhaps evoking images of shepherds and shepherdesses.

pentatonic scale
a scale of notes (q.v.), containing five notes instead of the usual eight in a western scale. There are wide gaps between the third and fourth, and fifth and first notes. The pentatonic scale is often used in classroom music-making. It can be easily found by playing just the black notes on a keyboard. However, pentatonic scales can be created starting on *every* note as follows:

C D E	G A	E F♯ G♯	B C♯	G♯ B♭ C	D♯ F
C♯ D♯ F	G♯ B♭	F G A	C D	A B C♯	E F♯
D E F♯	A B	F♯ G♯ B♭	C♯ D♯	B♭ C D	F G
D♯ F G	B♭ C	G A B	D E	B C♯ D♯	F♯ G♯

percussion section
the section of the orchestra containing instruments that are struck (and also the piano, whose strings are struck by felt-covered hammers).

phrase
a short section of melody (the musical equivalent of a phrase or clause in a sentence).

piano pedals
the right pedal (sustaining pedal) lifts the dampers from the strings and allows them to resonate freely; the left pedal (soft pedal or *una corda*) *either*

moves the hammers closer to the strings so that they cannot be struck so hard *or* moves the hammers to one side so that one string remains unstruck. Some large pianos have a middle pedal which allows a single chord to be sustained whilst other notes (normally damped) are played around it.

pitch

the height or depth of a sound, in Western music named by using one of the first seven letters of the alphabet.

pulse

see 'beat'.

rhythm

if you clap a tune instead of singing or playing it, you are clapping its rhythm.

roll

notes played on a drum as rapidly as possible, one after the other, to give the effect of continuous sound.

round

a piece of music in which the same tune is sung or played by two or more people starting one after another (e.g., 'London's burning,' 'Frère Jacques').

scale

a succession of adjacent notes going higher or lower.

score

the written-down version of a piece of music. When we see a poem printed in a book we are seeing the 'score' of the poem — the actual poem is what we hear when the words are read.

sharp (♯)

see 'Where the notes are to be found on a keyboard'.

small-pipes

Scottish version of Northumbrian pipes (q.v.), not to be confused with the mouth-blown Highland pipes.

string section

the group of orchestral instruments consisting of violin, viola, cello, and double bass. Guitar, banjo, ukelele, sitar, etc., are also string instruments (but not orchestral instruments). The piano is not (see percussion section).

structure

the way a piece of music is assembled from various different elements (sometimes called its 'form'). The shape of a piece.

suite

a number of different pieces of music played one after the other and considered to constitute one work. Originally a set of dances, nowadays often the best parts of a ballet or a musical played for listening to without dancing or action, e.g., a suite of pieces from *The Firebird* by Stravinsky (see **Just imagine**), or a suite of pieces from *West Side Story*.

swanee whistle

recorder-like instrument with a plunger that is pulled in and out to alter the note instead of holes for the fingers to cover.

symphony

a major musical work usually consisting of four movements (q.v.).

texture

I use the term texture in exactly the way we might talk about the texture of a piece of fabric. Instead of being rough, smooth, soft, etc., to the touch, a musical texture is rough, smooth, soft on the ear.

timbre

tone-colour (see 'colour').

trembling

I have used the word in the text instead of the Italian musical term, 'tremolando', which is used to instruct a string player to make the bow shiver rapidly back and forth across the string.

trill

the rapid alternation of two (usually adjacent) notes.

uilleann pipes

Irish bellow-blown bagpipes (sometimes called Union pipes), similar to Northumbrian and small-pipes but larger and with extra tubes called regulators that can add accompanying notes to the melody and drones.

unpitched/untuned

a sound or instrument without specific pitch or note (see 'pitch'), e.g., drum, maracas, tambourine.

variation

an elaboration or altered version of a musical idea. Composers write sets of variations in which a basic melody is first stated, then followed by a series of transformations. For examples listen to:

Rachmaninov *Variations on a theme of Paganini*
Dohnányi *Variations on a nursery theme*
Elgar *Enigma Variations*

vibraphone

a large metallophone with electrically driven resonators that make the notes vibrate. Like the marimba (q.v.), it is widely used in modern jazz as well as contemporary music.

woodwind section

the orchestral instruments that are made of wood (except the flute which is now usually made of metal) and are blown. They are piccolo (a miniature flute), flute, alto flute (a larger, deeper flute), oboe, cor anglais (a large oboe), E♭ clarinet (a miniature clarinet), clarinet, bass clarinet, bassoon, contra bassoon (a bass bassoon). Saxophones are occasional visitors to the orchestral woodwind section (e.g., in Ravel's *Bolero*), but are usually to be heard playing jazz.

xylophone

a series of tuned wooden (or plastic) bars on a resonating box (see glockenspiel).

Where the notes are to be found on a keyboard

Xylophones, metallophones, and glockenspiels have note names engraved on their bars. Chromatic instruments (i.e., those with *all* the notes) are arranged in two 'decks':

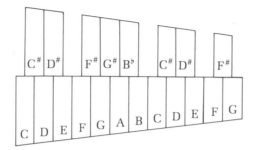

The notes on any keyboard correspond to the notes on a chromatic xylophone. The upper deck of the xylophone and the black notes of the piano are the same. They are arranged in alternate groups of two and three notes.

The white notes are named with the first seven letters of the alphabet. A is always found between the right hand two of a group of three black notes:

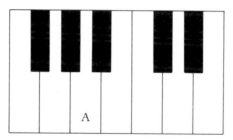

Moving to the right, the white notes are therefore A B C D E F G. The next is A again, and so forth, to the top of the keyboard.

Each black note has two names (although only one is normally engraved on the bars of a xylophone). It either takes the name of the white note to its left (one note lower) and adds the symbol ♯ (sharp), or takes the name of the white note to its right (one note higher), and adds the symbol ♭ (flat).

Thus the black note to the right of A is called either A♯ (A sharp) or B♭ (B flat).

Here is a complete scale of notes with their names:

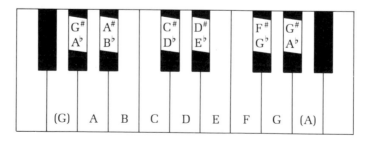